Table of Content

Table of Content 1
Chapter 1: Introduction 3
Chapter 2: Basic Sewing Techniques 17
Chapter 3: Simple Sewing Projects for Beginners 30
Chapter 4: Working with Patterns 41
Chapter 5: Sewing for the Home 55
Chapter 6: Sewing for Fashion.................................. 65
Chapter 7: Sewing for Kids 77
Chapter 8: Sewing for Special Occasions................. 86
Chapter 9: Advanced Sewing Techniques................. 97
Chapter 10: Exploring Different Fabric Types 108
Chapter 11: Embroidery and Decorative Stitches 120
Chapter 12: Patchwork and Quilting 131
Chapter 13: Sewing for Creativity 142
Chapter 14: Troubleshooting and Repairs 152
Chapter 15: Care and Maintenance 161
Chapter 16: Inspiration and Resources 168
Chapter 17: Developing Your Sewing Skills.............. 178

Chapter 18: Sewing for the Future 185

Chapter 19: Glossary of Terms 194

Chapter 20: Conclusion... 203

Chapter 1: Introduction

1.1: Welcome to the World of Sewing

In this comprehensive guide, we'll embark on an adventure that will unravel the secrets of sewing, empowering you to create stunning pieces that reflect your unique style and vision. We'll delve into the fundamentals of sewing, exploring the essential tools, materials, and techniques that will lay the foundation for your sewing endeavors. Join us as we stitch together a tapestry of knowledge and inspiration, guiding you on a path towards mastering this timeless craft.

Prepare to be captivated as we introduce you to a world where fabrics dance beneath your fingertips, threads become vibrant expressions of your creativity, and the sewing machine transforms into an extension of your imagination. Embrace the opportunity to unleash your inner artist, transforming ordinary materials into extraordinary creations that will adorn your life and inspire those around you.

Sewing, a craft that transcends time and cultures, offers a sanctuary for relaxation and a boundless avenue for personal growth. As you navigate the intricacies of sewing, you'll cultivate patience, precision, and a keen eye for detail. The act of sewing itself becomes a form of mindful meditation, allowing you to de-stress, focus on the present moment, and lose yourself in the rhythm of needle and thread.

So, dear aspiring seamstress or seasoned sewist, let's embark on this extraordinary adventure together. Allow your imagination to soar, embrace the transformative power of sewing, and discover the boundless possibilities that await you in this captivating world.

1.2: Why Sewing?

Embarking on the journey of sewing unlocks a realm of endless possibilities for personal expression, practical solutions, and therapeutic benefits. Sewing transcends the mere act of stitching fabric together; it empowers you to transform your ideas into tangible creations, fostering a sense of accomplishment and pride.

For those seeking a creative outlet, sewing offers a boundless canvas. With a needle and thread, you can paint vibrant tapestries of fabric, bringing your imagination to life. From delicate embroidery to bold patchwork designs, sewing allows you to explore your artistic side and express your unique style.

Beyond its creative appeal, sewing also serves practical purposes. Whether mending a torn garment, customizing an existing piece, or crafting functional items such as curtains or tote bags, sewing empowers you to take control of your wardrobe and household. By mastering the art of sewing, you gain the ability to extend the lifespan of your belongings and create personalized items that perfectly suit your needs.

Furthermore, the rhythmic motion of sewing has been shown to have therapeutic benefits. The act of manipulating fabric and guiding the needle through it can induce a sense of calm and reduce stress levels. As you focus on the present moment and engage in the repetitive movements of sewing, your mind can unwind and find solace.

In today's fast-paced society, where mass-produced goods often lack individuality, sewing offers a respite from the mundane. By creating your own sewn items, you not only gain a tangible sense of accomplishment but also foster a connection with your creativity and cultivate a sense of self-reliance. Whether you seek to mend, create, or simply unwind, sewing provides a rewarding and empowering path to fulfillment.

1.3: Essential Tools and Equipment

Embarking on a sewing journey necessitates equipping oneself with the proper tools and equipment to ensure a seamless and fulfilling experience. These tools serve as extensions of your hands, allowing you to manipulate fabric with precision and ease. From measuring to cutting, stitching to pressing, each tool plays a crucial role in transforming fabric into wearable art.

Measuring and Marking Tools

The accuracy of your sewing projects hinges upon precise measurements. A flexible measuring tape is indispensable for taking accurate measurements of fabric, while a ruler or T-square provides straight lines for measuring and marking seam allowances. Fabric marking pens or chalk in various colors allow you to clearly mark sewing lines and design details on the fabric.

Cutting Tools

Sharp, well-maintained cutting tools are essential for

clean, precise fabric cuts. A pair of fabric shears, designed specifically for cutting fabric, should be your go-to tool for most cutting tasks. Rotary cutters and cutting mats offer a faster and more efficient way to cut multiple layers of fabric accurately. Pinking shears, with their zigzag blade, prevent fraying on raw edges, making them ideal for finishing seams.

Sewing Machines

The sewing machine is the heart of any sewing setup. Choose a machine that aligns with your skill level and project needs. A basic mechanical machine is suitable for beginners, while a computerized model offers advanced features and stitch options. Regardless of the machine you choose, proper maintenance, including regular cleaning and oiling, is crucial for optimal performance.

Notions and Accessories

An assortment of sewing notions and accessories complements your sewing tools. Needles come in various sizes and types, each designed for specific fabrics and sewing techniques. Thread, available in a range of colors and weights, plays a vital role in holding your seams together. Pins and clips are used to hold fabric layers in place before stitching. A seam ripper allows you to undo stitches with ease, and a thimble protects your fingers while pushing needles through fabric.

Pressing Tools

Proper pressing is key to achieving a polished, professional-looking finish. An iron and ironing board are essential for pressing seams, shaping fabric, and removing wrinkles. A seam roller can help set seams firmly, while a pressing cloth protects delicate fabrics from scorching. A spray bottle filled with water can be used to lightly dampen fabrics, making them easier to press.

Additional Considerations

Beyond the essential tools listed above, consider your specific sewing interests and projects to determine any additional equipment you may need. For example, a serger can produce professional-looking finished edges, while an embroidery machine allows you to add intricate designs to your creations.

Remember, the best sewing tools are those that feel comfortable in your hands and enable you to work efficiently. With the right equipment and a little practice, you'll be well on your way to transforming fabric into beautiful, handmade treasures.

1.4: Understanding Fabric Types

Natural fibers, a gift from nature, have been the foundation of textiles for centuries. Cotton, a ubiquitous choice, captivates with its breathability, versatility, and unmatched comfort against the skin. Its inherent absorbency makes it ideal for garments that wick away moisture, keeping you cool and collected. Linen, another natural wonder, exudes an aura of understated elegance. Its exceptional strength and resistance to wrinkles render it a durable companion, perfect for home décor and summer attire. Silk, the epitome of luxury, drapes beautifully, offering a lustrous sheen and a soft, caressing touch. Its breathability and temperature-regulating properties make it a coveted fabric for garments and bedding. Wool, a natural insulator, shields against the cold with its warmth and moisture-wicking abilities. Its resilience and wrinkle resistance make it a practical choice for outerwear and tailoring.

Synthetic fibers, a product of scientific innovation, have revolutionized the textile industry. Polyester, a versatile workhorse, boasts strength, durability, and wrinkle resistance. Its moisture-wicking properties make it a favored choice for activewear and outdoor gear. Nylon, another synthetic marvel, is renowned for its exceptional strength and abrasion resistance. It finds its niche in luggage, backpacks, and swimwear. Acrylic, mimicking the warmth of wool, offers a soft, hypoallergenic alternative. Its resistance to fading and moths makes it a practical choice for sweaters, blankets, and plush toys. Spandex, with its remarkable elasticity, allows for a wide range of movement. It's commonly used in activewear, swimwear, and garments that demand a close, comfortable fit.

Blended fabrics, a harmonious marriage of natural and synthetic fibers, combine the best of both worlds. Cotton blends, for instance, retain the breathability and comfort of cotton while gaining added strength and wrinkle resistance from synthetic fibers. Linen blends offer a similar balance, with the added benefit of reduced creasing. Silk blends bring a touch of luxury to everyday fabrics, enhancing their drape and durability. Wool blends combine the warmth and insulation of wool with the easy care and wrinkle resistance of synthetics.

The choice of fabric for your sewing project hinges on several key considerations. The intended use of the garment or item plays a pivotal role. For garments that demand comfort and breathability, natural fibers like cotton and linen reign supreme. For durability and wrinkle resistance, synthetic fibers like polyester and nylon excel. When flexibility and stretch are paramount, spandex or spandex blends are the ideal choice. The drape and aesthetics of the fabric are equally important. Silky fabrics create elegant, flowing garments, while crisp fabrics like linen lend a structured, tailored look. The weight and thickness of the fabric must also be considered, as heavier fabrics are suitable for coats and upholstery, while lighter fabrics are ideal for summer wear and delicate projects.

With a discerning eye and a deep understanding of fabric types, you'll transform from a novice seamstress into a fabric connoisseur. Your creations will exude not only technical proficiency but also an innate sense of style and sophistication. So, embrace the world of fabrics, experiment with different types, and let your creativity soar to new heights.

1.5: The Sewing Machine Basics

From its humble beginnings in the 18th century to its present-day technological advancements, the sewing machine has undergone a remarkable transformation, revolutionizing the textile industry and empowering individuals to create and repair garments with unprecedented ease and precision. Early sewing machines, such as the one invented by Thomas Saint in 1790, employed a simple needle and shuttle mechanism to create a lockstitch, laying the foundation for future developments.

Elias Howe and the Lockstitch: A Pivotal Innovation

In 1846, Elias Howe's groundbreaking invention of the lockstitch sewing machine marked a significant turning point. His machine utilized two threads, one from above and one from below, to form a secure and durable stitch, vastly improving upon the chain stitch produced by earlier models. This innovation transformed the sewing machine from a novelty into a practical tool for both domestic and industrial applications.

Isaac Singer: The Commercialization and Refinement

Isaac Singer's 1851 sewing machine further refined the design, incorporating a foot pedal for hands-free operation, a tension adjuster to control stitch tightness, and a presser foot to hold the fabric in place. Singer's astute business acumen played a crucial role in popularizing the sewing machine, making it accessible to a wider audience through installment payment plans and aggressive marketing campaigns.

Modern Innovations: Technology at the Service of Sewing

The 20th century witnessed a flurry of technological advancements in the sewing machine industry. Electric motors replaced hand-cranking, providing consistent power and speed. Electronic controls allowed for precise stitch selection and adjustment, while computerized machines offered a wide range of automated features, from built-in stitch patterns to automatic thread trimming.

The Sewing Machine Today: A Versatile Creative Tool

Today, the sewing machine stands as a testament to human ingenuity and the transformative power of technology. It has evolved from a labor-intensive tool into a versatile creative companion, enabling individuals to express their creativity through a myriad of sewing projects, from basic repairs to elaborate garments and home décor items. The sewing machine continues to play a vital role in both the textile industry and personal endeavors, empowering individuals with the ability to create, mend, and customize their textiles with precision, efficiency, and a touch of artistry.

1.6: Getting Started: Your First Project

As a novice sewist embarking on your creative journey, your first project holds immense significance. It sets the stage for your sewing adventures and lays the foundation for your future endeavors. To ensure a successful and enjoyable experience, meticulous planning and preparation are crucial.

Before you delve into the practicalities of stitching, it is imperative to familiarize yourself with the essential tools and materials. Each component plays a specific role in the sewing process, and understanding their purpose will empower you to work efficiently and effectively. From selecting the right type of fabric to choosing the appropriate needles and thread, every detail matters.

Once your tools are assembled, it is time to choose your first project. Opt for a simple pattern that aligns with your skill level and interests. Avoid overly ambitious endeavors, as they can lead to frustration and discouragement. Begin with straightforward designs that allow you to practice basic stitches and techniques, such as a simple tote bag or a basic apron.

Before commencing any sewing project, it is essential to thoroughly read and comprehend the instructions. Take your time to familiarize yourself with the steps and ensure you have all the necessary materials. This thorough preparation will prevent costly mistakes and ensure a smooth workflow.

As you embark on your sewing journey, remember that practice makes perfect. The more you sew, the more proficient you will become. Embrace the learning process and do not be afraid to make mistakes. Each error is an opportunity to refine your skills and enhance your understanding of the craft.

Choosing the Right Fabric and Notions

Selecting the appropriate fabric for your first project is paramount. Consider factors such as the weight, drape, and texture of the material. For beginners, cotton is an excellent choice due to its versatility, ease of handling, and wide availability. Once you have chosen your fabric, it is time to gather the necessary notions. These include items such as thread, needles, scissors, measuring tape, and pins. Match the thread and needles to the weight and type of fabric you are using. Invest in quality notions as they will contribute significantly to the overall success of your project.

Preparing Your Fabric

Before you begin sewing, it is essential to prepare your

fabric properly. This involves prewashing and ironing it to remove any wrinkles or shrinkage that may occur during the sewing process. Prewashing will also help to set the colors and prevent fading. Once your fabric is prepared, it is ready to be cut and sewn.

Sewing Your First Project

Follow the instructions carefully and take your time. Do not rush the process, as this can lead to mistakes. If you encounter any difficulties, do not hesitate to consult a sewing book or online resources for guidance. Once you have completed your first project, take a moment to admire your accomplishment. Celebrate your success and reflect on the skills you have acquired.

Chapter 2: Basic Sewing Techniques

2.1: Threading the Machine

The proper threading of your sewing machine is crucial for successful sewing. Before you begin any project, take the time to carefully thread your machine according to the manufacturer's instructions. This will help to ensure that your stitches are even and secure, and that your fabric feeds through the machine smoothly.

Step-by-Step Guide to Threading Your Machine

1. Raise the presser foot. This will allow you to access the threading path more easily.
2. Insert the spool of thread onto the spool pin. The spool pin is usually located on the top of the machine. Make sure that the thread unwinds from the spool in a clockwise direction.
3. Pass the thread through the thread guide. The thread guide is a small metal loop that helps to keep the thread on track.

4. Pull the thread down through the tension discs. The tension discs are two metal discs that help to regulate the tension of the thread.
5. Hook the thread around the take-up lever. The take-up lever is a small metal arm that moves up and down as you sew.
6. Pass the thread through the needle. The needle is located in the needle bar. Make sure that the thread passes through the needle from front to back.
7. Pull the thread through the presser foot. The presser foot is a metal foot that holds the fabric in place as you sew.
8. Lower the presser foot. The presser foot will now hold the thread in place as you sew.

Troubleshooting Threading Problems

If you are having trouble threading your machine, there are a few things you can check:

Make sure that the thread is unwinding from the spool in a clockwise direction.
Check that the thread is passing through all of the thread guides correctly.
Make sure that the tension discs are not too tight or too loose.
If the thread is breaking, try using a different type of thread or a different needle.

Tips for Successful Threading

Use a good quality thread. Cheap thread is more likely to break or tangle.
Use the correct needle size for the fabric you are sewing. A too-small needle will not be able to penetrate the fabric properly, and a too-large needle will create large holes.
Thread your machine in a well-lit area. This will help you to see the threading path more clearly.
Be patient. Threading a sewing machine can be a bit tricky at first, but with practice, you will become more proficient.

2.2: Choosing the Right Needle and Thread

When it comes to sewing, the choice of needle and thread is crucial for achieving optimal results. Each type of fabric and sewing technique requires specific needles and threads to ensure proper stitching and fabric handling. Understanding the characteristics of different needles and threads empowers you to make informed decisions and enhance your sewing experience.

Needle Selection

Needles are characterized by their size, shape, and point style. The size refers to the diameter of the needle, with a higher number indicating a thinner needle. For most general-purpose sewing, needles in the range of 70. 10 to 90. 14 are suitable.

The shape of the needle determines its functionality. Round point needles are used for general sewing on woven fabrics, while ballpoint needles are ideal for knit fabrics as they prevent snagging. Sharp needles are designed for piercing tough materials like denim, and embroidery needles have a smaller eye to accommodate fine embroidery threads.

Thread Selection

Threads vary in fiber content, weight, and finish. The most common fiber types are cotton, polyester, and nylon. Cotton thread is natural, biodegradable, and absorbent, making it suitable for breathable fabrics like cotton and linen. Polyester thread is strong, durable, and resistant to fading, ideal for synthetic fabrics and outdoor projects. Nylon thread is particularly strong and elastic, making it excellent for sewing stretch fabrics.

The weight of thread refers to its thickness. Lighter threads are more delicate and suitable for fine fabrics, while heavier threads are more durable and suitable for heavier fabrics. The finish of thread can affect its appearance and functionality. Unfinished threads have a matte finish, while mercerized threads have a lustrous sheen and are stronger.

Matching Needle and Thread

To achieve the best stitching results, it's essential to match the needle and thread correctly. As a general rule, thicker threads require larger needles, while thinner threads require smaller needles. For example, a 70. 10 needle is suitable for cotton thread in the weight range of 30 to 40, while a 90. 14 needle is more appropriate for heavier threads like upholstery thread.

Additionally, the fabric type should also be considered when selecting the needle and thread. For woven fabrics, a sharp needle is recommended to pierce the fibers cleanly. For knit fabrics, a ballpoint needle is preferred to prevent snagging and maintain the fabric's elasticity. Delicate fabrics like silk require fine needles and threads to avoid damaging the fabric.

By understanding the different characteristics of needles and threads, you can confidently make informed choices that will elevate your sewing projects and ensure professional-looking results.

2.3: Basic Stitches: Straight Stitch, Zigzag Stitch, Backstitch

The straight stitch is the most basic and versatile stitch used in sewing. It is created by passing the needle through the fabric in a straight line, creating a series of evenly spaced stitches. The length of the stitch can be adjusted to create different effects, from fine and delicate to bold and sturdy. The straight stitch is suitable for a wide range of fabrics and sewing projects, from simple seams to intricate embroidery.

The zigzag stitch is a variation of the straight stitch that creates a series of zigzag-shaped stitches. This stitch is often used for finishing edges to prevent fraying, as well as for decorative purposes. The width and length of the zigzag stitch can be adjusted to create different effects, from a narrow, delicate finish to a wide, decorative edge. The zigzag stitch is also suitable for a wide range of fabrics, including lightweight and stretchy fabrics.

The backstitch is a strong and durable stitch that is created by sewing forward for a few stitches and then reversing the direction of the stitches. This creates a series of overlapping stitches that are very secure. The backstitch is often used for seams that need to be strong and durable, such as in garments or bags. It can also be used for decorative purposes, creating a unique and interesting texture. The backstitch is suitable for a wide range of fabrics, including heavy and durable fabrics.

2.4: Seam Allowance and Cutting Fabric

Heavier fabrics, such as denim or canvas, may require larger seam allowances of 3. 4 to 1 inch (1. 9 to 2. 5 centimeters) for added strength and durability. Conversely, lightweight fabrics, like chiffon or silk, may use narrower seam allowances of 1. 4 to 1. 2 inch (0. 6 to 1. 3 centimeters) to maintain their delicate drape.

Special seam finishes, such as French seams or Hong Kong seams, may require wider seam allowances to accommodate the extra fabric folds. Similarly, decorative seams, like topstitching or piping, often use wider seam allowances to create a more prominent visual effect.

Cutting fabric accurately is essential for achieving precise and professional-looking garments. Measuring and marking the fabric ensures that the cut pieces align correctly and match the pattern specifications. Use a measuring tape or ruler to measure the fabric and mark the cutting lines with tailor's chalk or a fabric marking pen.

When cutting curves, use sharp scissors or a rotary cutter with a curved blade to ensure a smooth and accurate cut. Hold the fabric taut while cutting to prevent distortion or stretching. For straight lines, use a ruler or a cutting mat with a grid to guide the cut. A rotary cutter and cutting mat are particularly efficient for cutting large pieces of fabric.

After cutting, check the cut pieces against the pattern pieces to ensure they are the correct size and shape. Make any necessary adjustments before proceeding to the sewing stage. Accurate fabric cutting lays the foundation for a well-constructed and properly fitting garment.

2.5: Pressing and Ironing

In the realm of sewing, pressing and ironing are indispensable techniques that elevate the quality of your creations. While often overlooked, these processes are crucial for achieving a crisp, polished look that sets your garments apart.

Pressing, using a hot iron without steam, helps to shape and mold fabric by removing wrinkles and setting seams. It is performed on the wrong side of the fabric to avoid creating a shiny or burnt surface. By gently pressing the iron over the fabric, you can define seam allowances, flatten darts, and create crisp edges.

Ironing, on the other hand, involves using a hot iron with steam to smooth out wrinkles and creases. It is typically done on the right side of the fabric to refresh the garment and remove any residual moisture. The steam helps to penetrate the fabric fibers, relaxing them and removing stubborn wrinkles.

Both pressing and ironing require precision and attention to detail to achieve optimal results. The correct temperature setting is essential for each type of fabric to avoid damage or scorching. Experimentation with a scrap piece of fabric before pressing or ironing on the actual garment is highly recommended.

When pressing seams, it is important to ensure that they are perfectly flat and aligned. Use a ruler or seam guide to ensure accuracy. Darts should be pressed from the wide end towards the point to create a smooth, tapered shape. Curves and corners require extra care and should be pressed using a curved or pointed iron tip.

Ironing should be done with a smooth, gliding motion

to avoid creating creases or dragging the fabric. Always iron with the grain of the fabric, following the direction of the weave, to prevent distortion. When ironing delicate fabrics, use a pressing cloth or low heat setting to avoid damage.

By incorporating pressing and ironing into your sewing routine, you will notice a significant improvement in the overall appearance of your garments. These techniques not only enhance the aesthetics but also ensure that your creations fit better and last longer. With a little practice and attention to detail, you can master the art of pressing and ironing and elevate your sewing skills to a new level.

2.6: Hand Sewing Techniques

Hand sewing, an ancient craft, remains a fundamental technique for many sewing projects. Whether mending a seam, attaching embellishments, or creating intricate details, hand sewing offers precision and flexibility. This one explores various hand sewing techniques, empowering beginners to confidently tackle a wide range of sewing projects.

Basic Stitches

The foundation of hand sewing lies in mastering basic

stitches. The running stitch, the most common, is used for temporary basting, gathering, and joining pieces of fabric. The back stitch, providing strength and durability, is ideal for seams and hems. The slip stitch, almost invisible, is perfect for hemming garments and joining fabrics with a seamless finish. These stitches form the building blocks for more complex techniques.

Advanced Stitches

Beyond basic stitches, a range of advanced stitches adds decorative and functional elements to sewing projects. The blanket stitch, resembling a chain of loops, creates a sturdy edge finish and embellishes borders. The satin stitch, known for its smooth, satin-like appearance, is used for filling in areas, creating appliqués, and adding decorative details. The cross-stitch, widely used in embroidery, consists of intersecting diagonal stitches, forming patterns and designs.

Embroidery and Appliqué

Hand sewing shines in the realm of embroidery and appliqué. Embroidery, the art of stitching decorative designs onto fabric, elevates sewing projects with intricate patterns, vibrant colors, and personal expression. Appliqué, involving the attachment of fabric shapes to a base fabric, adds visual interest, texture, and dimensionality to garments, quilts, and other creations. Hand sewing allows for precise control and customization, enabling sewers to create unique and expressive pieces.

Invisible Mending and Repairs

Hand sewing also excels in the art of invisible mending and repairs. By carefully matching threads and stitches, sewers can seamlessly repair torn seams, mend holes, and reinforce weakened areas. Techniques such as darning, a specialized form of stitching, allow for the reconstruction of damaged fabrics, restoring garments and textiles to their original condition. Hand sewing empowers individuals to extend the life of their cherished items and foster a spirit of sustainability.

Choosing Needles and Threads

The choice of needle and thread is crucial for successful hand sewing. Different needle sizes and shapes are designed for specific fabrics and stitches. Thicker fabrics require larger needles, while delicate fabrics demand finer needles. Threads vary in composition, weight, and color, influencing the strength, durability, and appearance of the finished product. By selecting the appropriate needle and thread, sewers ensure optimal results and enhance the overall quality of their sewing projects.

Chapter 3: Simple Sewing Projects for Beginners

3.1: Making a Pillowcase

A pillowcase is a simple and practical sewing project that is perfect for beginners. It is a great way to learn the basics of sewing, such as how to thread a needle, sew a straight stitch, and turn a hem. A pillowcase can also be a fun and creative project, as you can choose the fabric and design that you like.

To make a pillowcase, you will need the following materials:

1. 2 yard of fabric
Thread
A needle
Scissors
A sewing machine (optional)

If you are using a sewing machine, you will also need a bobbin.

Instructions:

1. Cut two pieces of fabric that are 20 inches by 30 inches.
2. Place the two pieces of fabric right sides together and sew around the edges, leaving a 4-inch opening on one side.
3. Turn the pillowcase right side out and insert a pillow.
4. Fold the edges of the opening inward and sew them together to close the pillowcase.

Tips:

If you are using a sewing machine, use a straight stitch with a stitch length of 2. 5.
If you are sewing by hand, use a backstitch to secure the stitches.
You can use any type of fabric to make a pillowcase, but cotton is a good choice because it is soft and easy to sew.
You can add embellishments to your pillowcase, such as lace, ribbons, or buttons.

Variations:

You can make a pillowcase in any size. Just adjust the measurements of the fabric pieces accordingly.
You can make a pillowcase with a flange by adding a

strip of fabric around the edges.

You can make a pillowcase with a zipper or buttons instead of a simple opening.

3.2: Sewing a Tote Bag

The type of fabric you select for your tote bag will significantly impact its durability, functionality, and aesthetic appeal. Consider factors such as the intended use of the bag, the desired weight and texture, and your personal style preferences. For a sturdy and durable tote that can withstand everyday use, opt for a tightly woven canvas or denim. For a lighter and more casual bag, choose a cotton or linen blend. If you're aiming for a more refined look, consider silk, satin, or velvet.

Preparing the Fabric:

Before you start sewing, it's essential to prepare the fabric properly to ensure a clean and professional finish. Begin by pre-washing and drying the fabric to remove any shrinkage or distortion. This will also help to set the dyes and prevent fading. Once the fabric is dry, iron it thoroughly to remove wrinkles and creases. If the fabric has a nap (such as velvet or corduroy), be sure to iron it in the direction of the nap.

Cutting the Fabric:

The precision of your fabric cutting will directly affect the overall appearance and functionality of your tote bag. Use a sharp rotary cutter and ruler to ensure straight lines and accurate measurements. Refer to the pattern instructions or create your own cutting guide to determine the dimensions and shape of the fabric pieces you need. Be sure to leave a seam allowance of at least 1. 2 inch (1. 27 cm) around all edges.

Assembling the Tote Bag:

With the fabric pieces cut and prepared, it's time to assemble the tote bag. Follow the pattern instructions carefully, starting with the bottom of the bag. Pin the fabric pieces together, right sides facing, and sew them together using a straight stitch. Repeat the process for the sides and handles of the bag. Once all the pieces are sewn together, turn the bag right side out and press it to give it a finished look.

Finishing Touches:

To complete your tote bag, add any desired embellishments or finishing touches. This could include adding a zipper or magnetic closure, sewing on pockets, or embroidering a personalized design. These details will enhance the functionality and style of your bag and make it uniquely your own.

3.3: Crafting a Simple Scarf

Once the fabric is chosen, the dimensions of the scarf come into play. The length and width will determine the overall size and shape of the finished product. Consider the intended purpose of the scarf – will it be worn as a cozy neck warmer or a stylish accessory. A standard scarf typically measures around 60-72 inches in length and 8-12 inches in width, but these dimensions can be adjusted to suit personal preferences.

The next step involves cutting the fabric. Precision is key to ensure a clean and professional-looking finish. Measure and mark the desired dimensions on the fabric, taking into account any seam allowances. Use a sharp pair of fabric scissors or a rotary cutter and a cutting mat for accurate cuts.

With the fabric cut, it's time to assemble the scarf. The simplest method is to sew the two ends together, creating a loop. However, for a more polished look, consider adding a hem to the edges of the scarf. A narrow hem, stitched close to the edge, will prevent fraying and give the scarf a refined appearance.

The choice of thread color is an opportunity to add a subtle touch of personalization. Opt for a thread that complements the fabric or creates a contrasting effect. Use a needle that is appropriate for the fabric weight and type.

As you embark on the sewing process, take your time and pay attention to detail. Neat and even stitches will enhance the overall quality of the finished scarf. If you encounter any difficulties, don't hesitate to consult sewing resources or seek guidance from experienced sewers.

Once the scarf is sewn, give it a gentle press to remove any wrinkles and set the stitches. This final step will complete the transformation of your fabric into a beautiful and functional accessory. Wear your handcrafted scarf with pride, knowing that you have mastered the art of simple sewing.

3.4: Creating a Fabric Coaster

Embark on a delightful sewing adventure with this comprehensive guide to creating your own stylish fabric coasters. These coasters, adorned with vibrant fabrics and intricate patterns, will elevate your home décor while protecting your surfaces from unsightly spills and condensation rings. Whether you're a seasoned seamstress or just starting your sewing journey, this guide will provide you with the essential knowledge and techniques to create coasters that are both functional and aesthetically pleasing.

Selecting the Perfect Fabric:

The choice of fabric for your coasters is a crucial step that will influence their overall look and feel. Opt for fabrics that are absorbent, durable, and aesthetically pleasing. Cotton, linen, and canvas are excellent choices as they absorb moisture effectively, are relatively easy to sew, and come in a wide range of colors and patterns. Consider the colors and patterns of your home décor when selecting fabrics to ensure a cohesive and stylish look.

Essential Materials:

Before embarking on your coaster-making adventure, gather the necessary materials: fabric, batting or interfacing, thread, a sewing machine, scissors, a ruler or measuring tape, and a pencil or fabric marker. Batting or interfacing adds an extra layer of absorption and structure to your coasters, making them more durable and effective. Choose a thread color that complements your fabric and ensures secure stitching.

Cutting and Preparing the Fabric:

Measure and cut two pieces of fabric for each coaster, ensuring they are the desired size and shape. For a standard square coaster, cut two 6-inch squares. If you prefer a different shape, such as a circle or hexagon, use a template or compass to draw the desired shape onto the fabric and cut it out. Cut a piece of batting or interfacing the same size as the fabric pieces.

Assembling the Coaster:

Place one piece of fabric right side up and center the batting or interfacing on top. Place the second piece of fabric on top, right side down, aligning the edges. Pin the layers together around the edges, ensuring they are secure. Sew around the edges of the coaster, leaving a small opening for turning.

Finishing Touches:

Turn the coaster right side out through the opening you left. Use a chopstick or blunt object to gently push out the corners and edges, ensuring a smooth and even shape. Top stitch around the edges of the coaster, close to the edge, to secure the opening and enhance the finished look. Your fabric coaster is now complete, ready to protect your surfaces and add a touch of personal style to your home.

Experiment with Different Fabrics and Designs:

Once you have mastered the basic technique, explore your creativity by experimenting with different fabrics and designs. Combine various patterns and colors to create unique and eye-catching coasters that reflect your personal style. Consider adding embellishments such as lace, ribbons, or beads to further enhance the visual appeal of your coasters.

The satisfaction of creating something beautiful and functional with your own hands is an unparalleled feeling. With this beginner-friendly guide, you can embark on a delightful sewing journey and create fabric coasters that will add a touch of elegance and practicality to your home. Remember, the possibilities are endless, so let your creativity soar and enjoy the process of crafting these charming and useful accessories.

3.5: Upcycling Old Clothes into New Creations

There are many different ways to upcycle old clothes, but some of the most popular methods include:

Refashioning: This involves taking an old garment and altering it to create a new piece of clothing. For example, you could turn an old pair of jeans into a skirt or a dress.

Embellishment: This involves adding new embellishments to an old garment to give it a new look. For example, you could add lace, beads, or embroidery to an old t-shirt or dress.

Patchwork: This involves sewing together pieces of old fabric to create a new piece of clothing. For example, you could create a quilt or a pillowcase using old scraps of fabric.

Upcycling old clothes is a great way to be creative and express your own personal style. It is also a great way to save money and reduce your environmental impact.

Here are some tips for upcycling old clothes:

Start with clothes that you no longer wear. This will help you to avoid wasting any clothes that you still like or need.

Be creative and experiment with different ideas. There are no rules when it comes to upcycling old clothes. Don't be afraid to make mistakes. Upcycling is a learning process, and you will likely make mistakes along the way.

Have fun. Upcycling old clothes should be a fun and enjoyable experience.

Upcycling old clothes is a great way to give your wardrobe a fresh new look while also reducing your environmental impact. By following these tips, you can create unique and stylish pieces that are one-of-a-kind.

Chapter 4: Working with Patterns

4.1: Understanding Pattern Instructions

Pattern instructions typically begin with a list of materials, including fabric, notions, and tools. Familiarize yourself with the fabric types, such as cotton, silk, or denim, and their appropriate uses. Notions include items like zippers, buttons, and thread, which add functionality and style to your garments. Tools, such as scissors, measuring tape, and a sewing machine, are essential for cutting, measuring, and assembling the fabric.

The next section of the pattern instructions focuses on preparing the fabric. This may involve washing, drying, and ironing the fabric to remove wrinkles and ensure accurate cutting. The instructions will also guide you on laying out the fabric and cutting out the pattern pieces. Pay close attention to the grainlines indicated on the pattern pieces, as they determine the direction in which the fabric should be cut to achieve the desired drape and stability.

Once the fabric pieces are cut, you'll move on to assembling the garment. The pattern instructions will guide you through each step, from sewing darts and seams to inserting zippers and finishing the edges. Each step is typically accompanied by clear diagrams or illustrations to aid in visualization. Follow the instructions carefully, taking note of the seam allowances and any specific techniques required.

Pattern instructions often include helpful tips and suggestions throughout the process. These can range from advice on choosing the right fabric for the project to troubleshooting common sewing problems. Don't hesitate to consult these tips as you work through the pattern, as they can save you time and frustration.

In a nutshell, the pattern instructions will guide you through finishing the garment. This may involve hemming the edges, adding buttons or other closures, and pressing the finished garment. The instructions will also provide care instructions for the garment, ensuring its longevity and maintaining its appearance.

Understanding pattern instructions is a skill that improves with practice. By carefully following the steps outlined in the pattern and familiarizing yourself with the common elements, you'll gain confidence and proficiency in sewing. Remember, the journey of sewing is filled with learning experiences, and each completed project brings you closer to mastering the craft.

4.2: Choosing the Right Pattern

One of the first steps in choosing the right pattern is to determine the type of garment you wish to create. Consider the occasion, personal style, and body type when selecting a pattern. For example, a formal gown will require a different pattern than a casual t-shirt. Similarly, patterns designed for specific body types, such as petite or curvy, can ensure a better fit and flatter your unique shape.

Once you have identified the type of garment you desire, it's time to delve into the specifics of the pattern. Pay attention to the pattern's description, which will provide details about the garment's style, fabric recommendations, and skill level required. If you are a beginner, it's advisable to start with patterns labeled as "easy" or "beginner-friendly. " These patterns typically feature simple construction techniques and clear instructions, making them less daunting for those new to sewing.

Another crucial factor to consider is the fabric you

intend to use. Different fabrics drape and behave in unique ways, so it's important to select a pattern that is compatible with your chosen fabric. The pattern description will usually include fabric suggestions, but it's always wise to consult with a fabric expert or conduct your own research to ensure the best match.

In a nutshell, don't hesitate to consult resources and seek guidance when making pattern selections. Sewing books, online forums, and experienced sewers can provide valuable insights and recommendations. By taking the time to understand the fundamentals of pattern selection, you can lay the foundation for successful and fulfilling sewing projects that will bring your creative visions to life.

4.3: Taking Accurate Body Measurements

Body measurements are crucial for ensuring that garments fit comfortably and flatter the wearer's figure. Accurate measurements are essential for pattern selection, alterations, and creating custom-made garments. Taking precise body measurements requires a measuring tape, a notepad, and a willing participant.

To obtain accurate body measurements, follow these steps:

- Choose a comfortable and well-lit space.
- Wear undergarments similar to those you will wear with the finished garment.
- Stand up straight with your feet shoulder-width apart and your arms relaxed at your sides.
- Inhale deeply and hold your breath momentarily to expand your chest. This will help ensure that the measurements are taken at the fullest point.
- Measure in inches or centimeters, depending on your preference. Record the measurements carefully on a notepad.

Bust Measurement

Wrap the measuring tape around the fullest part of your bust, ensuring it is parallel to the floor.
Hold the tape snugly, but not too tightly.
Read the measurement where the tape overlaps.

Waist Measurement

Find the natural waistline, which is typically the narrowest part of your torso.
Wrap the measuring tape around your waist, ensuring it is parallel to the floor.
Hold the tape snugly and read the measurement where the tape overlaps.

Hip Measurement

Stand with your feet together and measure around the fullest part of your hips.
Keep the measuring tape parallel to the floor and read the measurement where the tape overlaps.

Additional Measurements

In addition to the bust, waist, and hip measurements, other useful measurements include:

Shoulder to Waist: Measure from the top of your shoulder, over the highest point of your bust, to your natural waistline.
Shoulder to Hem: Measure from the top of your shoulder, down the center of your body, to the desired hem length.
Sleeve Length: Measure from the top of your shoulder, along the outside of your arm, to the desired sleeve length.
Inseam: Measure from the crotch seam to the bottom of your leg, along the inside seam of your pants or skirt.

Tips for Accuracy

Use a flexible measuring tape that conforms to the contours of your body.

Take measurements twice to ensure accuracy.

If possible, have someone else take your measurements to eliminate any bias.

Measure over undergarments to account for the thickness of clothing.

Stand up straight and avoid hunching or slouching.

Inhale deeply and hold your breath momentarily to ensure the measurements are taken at the fullest point.

Accurate body measurements are the foundation for successful sewing projects. By following these guidelines, you can ensure that your garments fit comfortably and flatter your figure.

4.4: Cutting and Laying Out Fabric

Before embarking on the cutting process, it is essential to prepare the fabric by ironing it thoroughly to remove any wrinkles or creases that could impede accurate cutting. This step also helps to stabilize the fabric and make it more manageable. Once the fabric is properly prepared, the pattern pieces can be arranged on the fabric's surface. Careful consideration should be given to the placement of the pattern pieces to minimize fabric waste and ensure the efficient use of materials.

When laying out the pattern pieces, it is important to pay attention to the direction of the fabric's nap, if applicable. Nap refers to the slight difference in texture or sheen on one side of the fabric compared to the other. Ensuring that all pattern pieces are aligned in the same direction of the nap creates a uniform appearance and enhances the overall aesthetic of the finished garment.

To ensure precision cutting, sharp scissors or a rotary cutter are indispensable tools. Sharp blades provide clean, straight cuts that prevent fraying and contribute to the garment's overall quality. When cutting, it is crucial to follow the pattern markings meticulously, including seam allowances and notches. Seam allowances are the extra fabric added around the edges of the pattern pieces, providing space for sewing and seam finishing. Notches are small, triangular cuts made into the fabric at specific points, serving as alignment guides when sewing different pieces together.

After cutting out the fabric pieces, it is essential to organize them systematically to prevent confusion and facilitate the sewing process. Grouping similar pieces together, such as bodice pieces or sleeve pieces, ensures that they are easily accessible when needed. Additionally, marking the fabric pieces with their corresponding pattern labels helps to maintain clarity and organization throughout the sewing project.

Understanding the techniques of cutting and laying out fabric is a foundational skill for any aspiring sewist. By mastering these techniques, you will lay the groundwork for successful and satisfying sewing projects that showcase your precision and craftsmanship.

4.5: Transferring Pattern Markings

Transferring pattern markings onto fabric accurately is essential for achieving precise sewing results. Various methods are available, each with its advantages and disadvantages, depending on the fabric type, pattern markings, and desired outcome. Understanding the different techniques and their suitability for specific fabrics and patterns empowers sewers to select the most appropriate method for their project.

Tracing Paper: Precision with Flexibility

Tracing paper is a versatile material for transferring pattern markings onto fabric. Its transparency allows for accurate tracing, ensuring precise pattern placement. Additionally, it is easily repositionable, facilitating corrections and adjustments as needed.

However, tracing paper can be prone to tearing and may not adhere well to certain fabrics, such as stretchy or delicate materials.

Transfer Paper: Accuracy and Convenience

Transfer paper, specifically designed for sewing patterns, offers a convenient and precise solution for marking fabric. It is coated with a carbon-based material that transfers markings onto fabric with a simple rubbing motion. Transfer paper comes in various colors, allowing sewers to choose one that contrasts with the fabric color for enhanced visibility. However, it can be sensitive to moisture and may require careful handling to prevent smudging or unintended marking.

Pinking: Visibility and Easy Removal

Pinking, using a rotary cutter or scissors with zigzag blades, creates small notches along pattern markings. These notches are easily visible and provide a clear guide for sewing or cutting. Pinking is particularly useful for fabrics that fray easily, as the zigzag edges prevent unraveling. However, it may not be suitable for delicate fabrics that could be damaged by the pinking process.

Tailor's Chalk: Temporary Marking with Flexibility

Tailor's chalk is a traditional method for marking fabric. It is available in various colors and can be easily applied with a chalk wheel or marker. Tailor's chalk is particularly useful for temporary markings that can be easily removed with brushing or washing. However, it may not be suitable for fabrics with dark or heavily textured surfaces, as the chalk may not show up clearly.

Embroidery Transfer Pen: Permanent and Decorative

Embroidery transfer pens, filled with a water-soluble ink, are specifically designed for transferring embroidery patterns onto fabric. They produce precise and permanent markings that can be sewn over. Embroidery transfer pens come in various colors and allow for intricate and decorative designs. However, they may not be suitable for fabrics that cannot withstand moisture or heat, as the markings require heat-setting to become permanent.

4.6: Sewing with Patterns

Sewing patterns provide a blueprint for creating garments and other textile projects. They include detailed instructions and precise measurements, enabling even beginners to achieve professional-looking results. Understanding the components of a pattern is essential for successful sewing.

The pattern envelope typically features an image of the finished product, along with a description of the garment's style, fabric requirements, and sizing information. Inside the envelope, you'll find pattern pieces made of thin paper or plastic, each representing a different part of the garment. These pieces are labeled with numbers or letters and have notches or symbols to indicate where they should be joined.

Choosing the Right Pattern

Selecting the appropriate pattern is crucial for a successful sewing project. Consider your skill level, the desired fit, and the type of fabric you plan to use. Pattern envelopes include a difficulty rating and a size chart to help you make an informed decision.

Preparing the Pattern

Before cutting out the fabric, you need to prepare the pattern. This involves checking the size and adjusting it if necessary, tracing the pattern pieces onto tracing paper or pattern marking paper, and cutting them out precisely.

Layout and Cutting

Once the pattern pieces are prepared, you can lay them out on the fabric and cut them out. It's important to follow the cutting lines carefully and pay attention to the grain lines, which indicate the direction of the fabric's fibers.

Assembling the Garment

With the fabric pieces cut out, you can begin assembling the garment. Sewing patterns typically provide step-by-step instructions that guide you through the process. Start by sewing the smaller pieces together, such as pockets and collars, before attaching them to the main body of the garment.

Fitting and Adjusting

Once the garment is assembled, it's time to try it on and make any necessary adjustments. Pin the garment closed and examine the fit. Adjust the seams or darts as needed to achieve the desired shape and size.

Finishing Touches

The final step is to finish the garment by adding

closures, such as zippers or buttons, and hemming the edges. Attention to detail during this stage will elevate the overall quality of your sewn project.

Benefits of Using Patterns

Using patterns offers several advantages:

Consistency: Patterns ensure that garments are made to a consistent size and shape, reducing the risk of errors.
Accuracy: Precise measurements and cutting lines help you achieve accurate and professional-looking results.
Simplicity: Even beginners can follow pattern instructions to create beautiful garments.
Customization: Patterns provide a framework that can be easily modified to create unique and personalized designs.
Professionalism: Using patterns helps you achieve a higher level of craftsmanship and a polished look in your sewing projects.

Chapter 5: Sewing for the Home

5.1: Curtains and Drapes

Curtains and drapes are an essential part of any home décor, providing both privacy and style. They can be made from a variety of fabrics, including sheer, voile, linen, velvet, and silk. The type of fabric you choose will depend on the desired look and feel of the room.

Sheer curtains are lightweight and airy, allowing natural light to filter through while still providing some privacy. They are a good choice for rooms that need a light and airy feel, such as living rooms and bedrooms. Voile curtains are similar to sheer curtains, but they are slightly heavier and have a more textured look. They are a good choice for rooms that need a bit more privacy, such as bathrooms and kitchens.

Linen curtains are made from natural fibers, which gives them a relaxed and casual look. They are a good choice for rooms that have a rustic or farmhouse style. Velvet curtains are luxurious and elegant, and they can add a touch of drama to any room. They are a good choice for formal rooms, such as dining rooms and living rooms. Silk curtains are the most luxurious type of curtain, and they can add a touch of opulence to any room. They are a good choice for special occasions, such as weddings and parties.

In addition to the fabric, you will also need to choose the right curtain rod. The type of curtain rod you choose will depend on the weight of the curtains and the desired look of the room. For lightweight curtains, you can use a simple tension rod. For heavier curtains, you will need a more substantial curtain rod that is mounted to the wall or ceiling.

Once you have chosen the fabric and curtain rod, you can begin sewing your curtains. The process is relatively simple, and it can be completed in a few hours. First, you will need to measure the window and determine the desired length of the curtains. Then, you will need to cut the fabric to the desired size. To summarize, you will need to sew the fabric together and attach it to the curtain rod.

With a little bit of effort, you can create beautiful curtains and drapes that will add style and privacy to your home.

5.2: Tablecloths and Placemats

Tablecloths and placemats are essential components of any well-set table, adding both functionality and aesthetic appeal. They protect table surfaces from spills and scratches while creating a warm and inviting ambiance.

Choosing the right tablecloth or placemat depends on several factors, including the size and shape of the table, the occasion, and personal style. Tablecloths come in various materials, such as cotton, linen, silk, and lace, each with its unique characteristics and suitability for different settings. Placemats, typically smaller in size, are designed to accommodate individual diners and protect the tabletop directly beneath their dishes.

The size of the tablecloth is crucial to ensure proper fit. It should extend evenly over the edges of the table, with an overhang of approximately 6-12 inches on all sides. Placemats, on the other hand, should be large enough to accommodate the plate, utensils, and napkin, leaving ample space for comfortable dining.

The shape of the tablecloth or placemat should complement the table's shape. Rectangular tablecloths are ideal for rectangular or square tables, while round tablecloths suit circular tables. Oval tablecloths are available for oval tables, while custom shapes can be created to fit unique table designs.

The occasion also influences the choice of tablecloth or placemat. Formal events call for elegant materials like silk or linen in neutral colors or subtle patterns. For everyday use, cotton or other durable fabrics in vibrant colors or bold patterns can create a cheerful atmosphere.

Personal style plays a significant role in selecting tablecloths and placemats. They can reflect the homeowner's taste and preferences, adding a touch of personality to the dining experience. Whether it's traditional patterns, contemporary designs, or whimsical motifs, the choice should complement the overall decor of the dining room.

By considering these factors, individuals can create a harmonious and inviting dining space that showcases their style and enhances the enjoyment of every meal. Tablecloths and placemats are more than just functional items; they are versatile accessories that add a touch of elegance and warmth to any home.

5.3: Pillow Covers and Cushions

When choosing fabric for pillow covers, consider the overall style of your home décor. If you have a modern home, you might want to choose a solid-colored fabric or a fabric with a simple pattern. If you have a more traditional home, you might want to choose a fabric with a more elaborate pattern or a fabric with a texture.

Once you have chosen your fabric, you will need to cut it to the correct size. The size of the pillow cover will depend on the size of your pillow insert. You will also need to decide whether you want to make a pillow cover with a zipper or a flap closure.

If you are making a pillow cover with a zipper, you will need to sew the zipper into the side seam of the pillow cover. If you are making a pillow cover with a flap closure, you will need to sew the flap to the back of the pillow cover.

Once you have sewn the pillow cover, you can insert your pillow insert. You can then add any decorative touches you like, such as tassels, fringe, or embroidery.

Cushions are another great way to add comfort and style to your home. They can be used on sofas, chairs, beds, and even on the floor. Cushions are also relatively easy to make, and you can use any fabric you like.

When choosing fabric for cushions, consider the overall style of your home décor and the purpose of the cushion. If you are making a cushion for a sofa or chair, you might want to choose a durable fabric that is easy to clean. If you are making a cushion for a bed, you might want to choose a softer fabric that is more comfortable to sleep on.

Once you have chosen your fabric, you will need to cut it to the correct size. The size of the cushion will depend on the size of your cushion insert. You will also need to decide whether you want to make a cushion with a zipper or a flap closure.

If you are making a cushion with a zipper, you will need to sew the zipper into the side seam of the cushion. If you are making a cushion with a flap closure, you will need to sew the flap to the back of the cushion.

Once you have sewn the cushion, you can insert your cushion insert. You can then add any decorative touches you like, such as tassels, fringe, or embroidery.

Pillow covers and cushions are a great way to add personality to your home décor. They are relatively easy to make, and you can use any fabric you like. With a little creativity, you can create beautiful and unique pillow covers and cushions that will add comfort and style to your home.

5.4: Sewing Kitchen Accessories

One of the most practical and versatile kitchen accessories is the pot holder. These quilted squares or rectangular pieces of fabric protect your hands from heat while handling hot pots and pans. You can create pot holders using a variety of fabrics, such as cotton, canvas, or heat-resistant materials like Nomex or Kevlar. Quilting the fabric layers together adds an extra layer of insulation and durability.

Oven mitts are essential for protecting your hands when reaching into a hot oven. Similar to pot holders, oven mitts are typically made from heat-resistant fabrics and feature a quilted or insulated design. You can add a personal touch to your oven mitts by choosing fabrics that complement your kitchen décor or by embellishing them with embroidery or appliqué.

Tablecloths and napkins are not only decorative but also functional accessories for your kitchen or dining room. A well-chosen tablecloth can set the mood for a special occasion or create a cozy atmosphere for everyday meals. You can sew tablecloths from a variety of fabrics, including cotton, linen, or lace. Napkins, on the other hand, are smaller versions of tablecloths and can be used to protect clothing while dining or to add a touch of elegance to your table setting.

Sewing kitchen accessories not only enhances the functionality and aesthetics of your kitchen but also provides an opportunity for creative expression. Whether you choose to create simple pot holders or elaborate tablecloths, the process of sewing these items allows you to personalize your home and add a touch of handmade charm to your everyday life.

In addition to their practical and aesthetic benefits, sewing kitchen accessories can also be a cost-effective way to upgrade your kitchen. By making your own pot holders, oven mitts, tablecloths, and napkins, you can save money compared to purchasing similar items from retail stores. Moreover, sewing these accessories allows you to control the quality of materials and craftsmanship, ensuring that you end up with durable and long-lasting items.

As you embark on your journey of sewing kitchen accessories, remember that the most important aspect is to enjoy the process and let your creativity shine through. With a little patience and practice, you'll be able to create beautiful and functional accessories that will bring joy to your kitchen for years to come.

5.5: Creating Decorative Wall Hangings

Choosing the right fabric for your wall hanging is a crucial step that sets the foundation for its overall aesthetic appeal. Consider the texture, color, and pattern of the fabric, ensuring it complements your existing décor or serves as a striking focal point. Experiment with different fabrics to achieve various effects, such as a soft and ethereal look with sheer fabrics or a bold and graphic statement with patterned canvas. The possibilities are limitless, and the choice is ultimately yours to make.

Once you've selected your fabric, it's time to decide on the design of your wall hanging. This is where your imagination can truly soar. Will it be a simple geometric shape, an intricate patchwork design, or perhaps a free-form composition inspired by nature. The possibilities are endless, so let your creativity guide you. Sketch out your design on paper first to visualize your concept and ensure its proportions are balanced.

The actual sewing process for a wall hanging is relatively straightforward. Start by cutting out the fabric pieces according to your design. If your design incorporates multiple pieces, carefully sew them together using a basic stitch, such as a straight stitch or zigzag stitch. Once the fabric is assembled, it's time to add any embellishments you desire. This could include beads, sequins, embroidery, or even three-dimensional elements like tassels or fringe. Let your creativity shine through as you personalize your wall hanging with unique details that reflect your style.

To complete your wall hanging, you'll need to attach a rod or dowel for hanging. This can be done by sewing loops or tabs onto the top of the fabric or using a more elaborate method like creating a channel for the rod to slide through. Once the hanging mechanism is in place, you can proudly display your handmade creation on your wall. The joy of creating something unique and beautiful is immeasurable, and every time you look at your wall hanging, you'll be reminded of your creative accomplishment.

Chapter 6: Sewing for Fashion

6.1: Basic Garment Construction

At the outset of garment construction, meticulous planning and preparation are paramount. Selecting suitable fabrics, patterns, and notions lays the groundwork for successful sewing projects. Fabric choice hinges upon the intended purpose of the garment, considering factors such as drape, texture, and durability. Patterns provide a blueprint for cutting and assembling the fabric pieces, ensuring accurate and consistent results. The judicious selection of notions, such as zippers, buttons, and thread, complements the fabric and pattern choices, contributing to the garment's functionality and aesthetic appeal.

Once the materials are assembled, the cutting process commences. Precise fabric cutting is crucial for achieving a professional-looking garment. Following the pattern instructions meticulously, the fabric is spread out smoothly and pinned securely to prevent shifting during cutting. Sharp scissors or a rotary cutter ensure clean, accurate cuts that align precisely with the pattern pieces.

With the fabric cut, the next step involves assembling the garment pieces. This entails sewing the pieces together in the correct order and orientation, guided by the pattern instructions. Various sewing techniques are employed, such as straight stitching, zigzag stitching, and overcasting, each serving a specific purpose in securing the seams and finishing the edges.

As the garment takes shape, meticulous attention to detail becomes increasingly important. Proper seam allowances are maintained throughout the sewing process, ensuring a consistent and professional finish. Trimming excess threads, pressing seams, and topstitching where necessary enhance the garment's overall quality and durability.

The final step in garment construction involves attaching closures, such as zippers, buttons, or hooks and eyes. These closures not only fasten the garment but also contribute to its functionality and style. Careful placement and secure attachment ensure the closures operate smoothly and withstand regular use.

Mastering garment construction techniques empowers

sewists to create a vast array of garments, from simple skirts to tailored jackets. With practice and patience, aspiring sewists can transform their fabric choices into wearable pieces that reflect their unique style and creativity.

6.2: Sewing a Skirt

Creating a stylish and well-fitting skirt is a fundamental skill in fashion sewing. This one delves into the intricacies of skirt construction, providing a comprehensive guide for beginners to master this essential garment.

Choosing Fabric and Pattern

The choice of fabric and pattern plays a crucial role in determining the final outcome of your skirt. Consider the drape, weight, and texture of the fabric, as well as the desired silhouette and occasion. Choose a pattern that complements your body shape and measurements.

Cutting the Fabric

Precise fabric cutting is essential for ensuring a professional finish. Carefully lay out the fabric and pattern pieces, ensuring proper grain alignment. Cut accurately along the marked lines, using sharp scissors or a rotary cutter.

Assembling the Skirt

The assembly process involves connecting the skirt pieces in the correct order. Start by sewing the side seams, matching the notches or markings. Insert the zipper or waistband closure, ensuring proper alignment and function. Next, attach the waistband to the top of the skirt, creating a secure and comfortable fit.

Finishing Touches

To complete your skirt, add finishing touches such as a hem, belt loops, or embellishments. The hem helps prevent fraying and creates a polished look. Belt loops provide functionality and style, while embellishments can add a personal touch.

Fitting and Adjustments

Once the skirt is assembled, try it on to assess the fit. Make necessary adjustments to the length, waistline, or hip area. If needed, take in or let out the seams to achieve a flattering and comfortable fit.

Troubleshooting Common Mistakes

Even experienced sewers can encounter challenges when sewing a skirt. Common mistakes include uneven seams, gaping waistbands, and fabric distortion. By understanding the potential pitfalls and their solutions, you can prevent or correct these issues.

Creating a skirt requires precision, creativity, and attention to detail. By following the instructions outlined in this one, you will gain the skills and confidence to design and sew your own stylish and well-fitting skirts. Remember to practice patience and enjoy the process of transforming fabric into wearable art.

6.3: Creating a Simple Blouse

When selecting fabric for a simple blouse, consider the desired drape, texture, and breathability. Lightweight woven fabrics like cotton voile, silk georgette, or rayon challis provide a fluid and flattering silhouette. For a more structured look, opt for crisp fabrics like linen or poplin. To determine the fabric yardage needed, measure your bust and hip circumferences. Multiply the bust measurement by 1. 5 to calculate the front fabric length and the hip measurement by 1. 5 to calculate the back fabric length. Add 1 yard for seam allowances and any design details like ruffles or pleats.

Pattern Layout and Cutting

Once you have the fabric, fold it in half with the selvages aligned. Pin the pattern pieces to the fabric, aligning the grainline arrows with the fabric's lengthwise grain. Cut out the front and back pieces, ensuring to follow the cutting lines carefully. If the blouse includes any sleeves, cut them out as well.

Shoulder and Side Seams

Begin sewing the blouse by pinning the front and back shoulder seams right sides together. Stitch the seams using a 5. 8-inch seam allowance. Press the seams open and finish the raw edges with a serger or zigzag stitch. Next, pin the side seams right sides together and stitch them with a 5. 8-inch seam allowance. Press the seams open and finish the raw edges.

Sleeves (Optional)

If the blouse includes sleeves, insert them by pinning the sleeve cap to the armhole of the blouse right sides together. Sew the seam with a 5. 8-inch seam allowance. Press the seam open and finish the raw edges. Topstitch around the armhole, about 1. 8-inch from the seam line, to secure the sleeve and create a decorative detail.

Neckline and Hem

Finish the neckline by sewing a narrow bias tape or ribbon around the raw edge. Fold the tape in half and pin it to the neckline, aligning the raw edges. Stitch the tape in place, close to the inner edge of the fold. Press the seam allowance away from the neckline and topstitch around the edge of the bias tape for a clean finish. To hem the blouse, fold up the bottom edge by 1 inch and press. Fold up another 1 inch and press again. Topstitch around the hem, about 1. 8-inch from the folded edge.

Finishing Touches

Once the blouse is sewn, add any desired embellishments, such as buttons, lace, or embroidery. If the blouse includes a zipper, insert it into the center back seam. Iron the blouse and hang it to dry before wearing.

6.4: Making a Dress

Mastering the art of dressmaking requires an in-depth understanding of construction techniques. These techniques form the foundation upon which a well-crafted dress is built. The process begins with selecting the appropriate fabric, which should complement the design and drape elegantly. Different fabrics possess unique properties, such as weight, texture, and stretch, which must be considered during construction.

Choosing the Right Sewing Machine and Tools

The choice of sewing machine plays a crucial role in the success of a dressmaking project. Whether opting for a mechanical or computerized machine, ensure it offers the necessary features and stitches for the project. Additionally, having the right tools, such as needles, thread, scissors, and measuring tools, is essential for precise and efficient sewing.

Preparing the Fabric and Pattern

Before cutting into the fabric, it must be properly prepared to prevent shrinkage or distortion. This involves prewashing and pressing the fabric to remove any wrinkles or impurities. The pattern pieces, which serve as templates for cutting the fabric, need to be carefully laid out and cut with precision to ensure accurate assembly.

Assembling the Dress

The assembly process involves joining the various pattern pieces together, starting with the bodice and working down to the skirt. Techniques such as darts, seams, and zippers are employed to create the desired shape and fit. Attention to detail is paramount at this stage, ensuring that seams are straight, stitches are even, and the overall construction is flawless.

Finishing Touches

Once the dress is assembled, the finishing touches complete its look. This may include hemming the edges, adding embellishments such as buttons, beads, or lace, and pressing the entire garment to give it a polished appearance. The finishing touches should complement the overall design and enhance the aesthetic appeal of the dress.

Tips for Success

To achieve success in dressmaking, it is important to follow certain guidelines. These include reading the pattern instructions carefully, measuring and cutting accurately, using the correct sewing techniques, and taking your time. Patience and attention to detail are key to creating a well-made dress that will last for years to come.

6.5: Designing and Customizing Garments

Designing and customizing garments is an art form that requires a blend of creativity, technical skills, and an understanding of fashion principles. The first step is to determine the purpose of the garment, whether it's for everyday wear, special occasions, or a particular style statement. Consider the target audience, their body type, and the occasion for which the garment will be worn. Once the design concept is established, it's crucial to gather inspiration from various sources such as fashion magazines, runway shows, and online platforms.

Selecting and Understanding Fabrics

The choice of fabric plays a pivotal role in the overall appearance and functionality of the garment. Different fabrics possess unique properties, textures, and drape, which can greatly influence the design. Common fabric types include cotton, linen, silk, wool, and synthetic blends. Understanding the characteristics of each fabric is essential, as some are suitable for tailored garments, while others lend themselves better to flowing designs. Fabric weight, texture, and color also need to be considered in relation to the design concept.

Drafting and Pattern Making

Pattern making is the process of creating a template that outlines the shape and dimensions of the garment. It involves taking measurements, creating a pattern, and adjusting it to achieve the desired fit and style. Patterns can be drafted from scratch or purchased pre-made. For beginners, using commercial patterns is a good starting point, as they provide a basic framework to work from. However, customizing patterns is essential to achieve a personalized fit and unique design elements.

Cutting and Sewing Techniques

Once the pattern is finalized, it's time to cut out the fabric pieces. Precision is crucial at this stage to ensure accuracy in the final assembly. Various cutting techniques exist, depending on the fabric type and the desired effect. Sewing techniques also vary depending on the fabric and the seam type. Hand sewing is often used for delicate fabrics or intricate details, while machine sewing is more efficient for larger garments. Understanding the proper sewing techniques is essential to achieve a professional-looking finish.

Customizing and Embellishing

The final stage of garment construction involves customizing and embellishing the garment to enhance its uniqueness. This can involve adding trims, such as lace, zippers, or buttons, as well as decorative elements like embroidery, beading, or appliqué. Customization allows you to express your personal style and create a garment that truly reflects your individuality. Embellishments can be subtle or elaborate, depending on the desired effect and the occasion for which the garment will be worn.

Chapter 7: Sewing for Kids

7.1: Sewing Toys and Stuffed Animals

Selecting the right fabrics for your toys is of paramount importance. Soft, cuddly materials like fleece, flannel, and plush fabrics are ideal for creating huggable companions. For added durability, consider using cotton or canvas fabrics for garments and accessories. Choosing fabrics with captivating patterns and vibrant colors will further enhance the visual appeal of your toys.

Before embarking on your sewing journey, it's essential to familiarize yourself with the basic tools of the trade. A sewing machine, needles, thread, scissors, and measuring tape are indispensable. Invest in quality tools that will ensure precise and efficient sewing. Additionally, specialized tools like embroidery needles and stuffing tools can elevate your creations.

Mastering the art of sewing seams is crucial for constructing durable and visually appealing toys. The most common types of seams used in toy making include the straight stitch, zigzag stitch, and blind stitch. Experiment with different stitch lengths and tensions to achieve the desired look and functionality. Reinforcing seams by backstitching or using a double stitch adds strength and longevity to your toys.

Creating patterns for your toys allows you to customize their size, shape, and features. You can either draft your own patterns or utilize pre-made patterns available online or in craft stores. When drafting patterns, pay meticulous attention to measurements and seam allowances to ensure a perfect fit. Trace patterns onto fabric using tracing paper, dressmaker's carbon paper, or a fabric marker.

Assembling your toys requires careful attention to detail and precision. Pin fabric pieces together accurately before sewing to prevent misalignment. Use small, sharp scissors to trim excess fabric and create clean edges. Stuffing your toys evenly and firmly gives them a plump and cuddly appearance. Insert safety eyes or embroidered details to add character and expression.

Finishing touches enhance the overall appeal and durability of your toys. Embroider names or personal touches to make them extra special. Add ribbons, bows, or buttons for embellishment and play value. Reinforce high-stress areas like joints and limbs with additional stitching or fabric reinforcement. Laundering instructions should be attached to ensure proper care and longevity.

By embracing the techniques and tips outlined in this comprehensive guide, you'll be well-equipped to embark on the enchanting journey of sewing toys and stuffed animals. These adorable creations will not only bring boundless joy to your children but also serve as cherished keepsakes that will be treasured for years to come. So, gather your materials, let your creativity soar, and experience the immense satisfaction of crafting handmade toys filled with love and laughter.

7.2: Making Baby Clothes

Creating baby clothes is a rewarding endeavor that allows sewers to express their creativity while crafting special and practical items for their little ones. By customizing store-bought garments or creating original designs from scratch, sewers can add personal touches that make each piece truly unique and meaningful.

One popular method for customizing baby clothes is through embellishments. Adding ribbons, lace, or embroidery to plain garments can transform them into eye-catching and stylish outfits. Sewers can also use fabric paints or markers to create unique designs or add special messages. These embellishments not only enhance the aesthetic appeal of the clothes but also create sentimental value, as they can be personalized to reflect the child's personality or interests.

Another way to make baby clothes more special is through fabric choice. Selecting soft, breathable fabrics such as cotton, muslin, or bamboo ensures the comfort of the baby while also providing opportunities for creative expression. Different fabrics can evoke different moods and styles, from delicate and feminine to playful and adventurous. By experimenting with various fabrics, sewers can create a range of garments that suit the individual needs and preferences of the baby.

In addition to aesthetics, sewers should also prioritize functionality when making baby clothes. Choosing durable fabrics and sturdy closures, such as snaps or zippers, ensures that the garments can withstand frequent wear and tear. Adding features such as adjustable waistbands or expandable necklines allows the clothes to grow with the baby, extending their lifespan and maximizing their value. By considering both style and practicality, sewers can create baby clothes that are not only beautiful but also practical and long-lasting.

When sewing for babies, it is essential to follow proper safety guidelines. All materials used, including fabrics, trims, and fasteners, should be non-toxic and safe for the baby's delicate skin. Avoid using sharp or loose embellishments that could pose a hazard to the child. Additionally, sewers should carefully check all seams and closures to ensure that they are secure and free from any potential defects that could compromise the baby's safety.

7.3: Creating Child-Sized Accessories

When sewing for kids, it's crucial to consider their unique proportions and requirements. Adapting adult-sized patterns or creating child-sized accessories from scratch requires careful attention to details. This guide provides comprehensive instructions for creating various child-sized accessories, including headbands, hats, and backpacks, to ensure a perfect fit and maximum comfort for your little ones.

For headbands, start by measuring the child's head circumference and adding 1-2 inches for overlap. Choose a soft, stretchy fabric that will gently hug the head without causing discomfort. Cut a strip of fabric to the desired length and width, and secure the ends together with an elastic band or sew them together. Embellish the headband with ribbons, beads, or appliqués to match the child's personality and style.

When making hats, consider the child's age and head size. For younger children, a simple beanie or sun hat with a brim is a practical choice. Measure the child's head circumference and add 2-3 inches for ease. Cut a circle of fabric for the crown and a rectangle for the brim. Sew the pieces together and secure with a chin strap or elastic band for a snug fit. For older children, experiment with different hat styles such as baseball caps, bucket hats, or floppy hats, and adjust the pattern accordingly.

Backpacks are a versatile accessory for both school and play. Choose a durable fabric that can withstand daily wear and tear. Start by creating a rectangular body for the backpack, adding a zipper or drawstring for closure. Sew on adjustable straps for comfort and convenience. Consider adding additional features such as exterior pockets, mesh panels, or reflective strips to enhance functionality and safety.

Remember to select fabrics that are soft, breathable, and appropriate for the child's age and intended use. Pay attention to details such as seam allowances, closures, and embellishments to ensure a high-quality and aesthetically pleasing finish. By following these guidelines, you can create a range of child-sized accessories that will bring joy and practicality to your little ones' lives.

7.4: Fun and Educational Sewing Projects

Engage young minds with the joy of sewing and ignite their creativity with a range of fun and educational projects. Sewing offers a myriad of benefits, fostering fine motor skills, problem-solving abilities, and a sense of accomplishment. These projects are carefully designed to spark curiosity and imagination while introducing essential sewing techniques.

Whimsical Animal Friends: Transform scraps of fabric into adorable animal puppets or cuddly toys. Encourage children to choose their favorite creatures and explore the textures and patterns of different fabrics. Introduce basic stitches like running stitch and backstitch to bring their animal friends to life.

Personalized Drawstring Bags: Create practical and stylish drawstring bags adorned with unique designs and patterns. Let children choose fabrics that reflect their interests and personality. They can practice measuring, cutting, and sewing straight lines to craft a bag that's both functional and expressive.

Fabric Mosaics: Encourage artistic expression with colorful fabric mosaics. Use small scraps of fabric to create intricate designs on a canvas or frame. Guide children through the process of piecing together fabrics and securing them with glue or stitches. This activity fosters pattern recognition and color theory concepts.

Upcycled T-Shirt Quilts: Transform old T-shirts into cherished memories with a cozy T-shirt quilt. Children can select their favorite shirts and cut them into squares, learning about symmetry and geometric shapes. Teach them the basics of quilting by sewing the squares together into a patchwork masterpiece.

Felt Food Creations: Engage children's imagination with playful felt food creations. Guide them through cutting out shapes from felt and assembling them with simple stitches. Encourage creativity by allowing them to invent their own dishes and explore the concept of pretend play.

Personalized Aprons: Foster independence and creativity by guiding children in sewing their own aprons. They can choose fabrics that match their kitchen or craft space and learn the basics of machine sewing. This project not only teaches practical skills but also encourages self-expression and responsibility.

Recycled Fabric Bookmarks: Transform old fabric scraps into useful and decorative bookmarks. Teach children the importance of recycling by showing them how to cut and stitch fabric pieces to create unique and personalized designs. Encourage them to experiment with different stitches and embellishments.

These fun and educational sewing projects offer a delightful way to engage children's creativity, develop their fine motor skills, and foster a love for sewing. By providing a variety of projects tailored to different ages and interests, you can empower young minds and inspire a lifelong passion for the craft of sewing.

Chapter 8: Sewing for Special Occasions

8.1: Creating Wedding Accessories

This comprehensive one delves into the intricacies of crafting veils, headpieces, and other adornments that will enhance the beauty and elegance of any bridal ensemble.

Veil-Making Techniques

The ethereal beauty of a wedding veil adds an air of mystery and romance to the bride's attire. Explore various techniques for creating veils, including hand-sewing, machine-stitching, and the use of lace trims. From classic cathedral veils to intricate fingertip veils, learn the steps involved in shaping, embellishing, and securing these graceful accessories.

Headpiece Crafting

Adorn the bride's coiffure with captivating headpieces that complement her personal style and the overall theme of the wedding. Discover the secrets of crafting stunning headbands, tiaras, and fascinators. Learn how to incorporate beads, crystals, and other embellishments to create pieces that are both elegant and eye-catching.

Other Accessories

In addition to veils and headpieces, a myriad of other accessories can enhance the bridal ensemble. Explore the art of sewing garters, corsages, and ring bearer pillows. Learn the techniques for creating these delicate items, ensuring they are not only beautiful but also functional.

Fabric and Material Selection

The choice of fabrics and materials plays a crucial role in the quality and aesthetic appeal of your wedding accessories. Understand the properties of different fabrics, such as silk, organza, and lace, and learn how to select the ideal materials for each project. Explore the vast array of embellishments, including beads, sequins, and pearls, and discover how to incorporate them tastefully into your designs.

Finishing and Detailing

The final touches transform ordinary accessories into extraordinary works of art. Learn the techniques for finishing and detailing, including hand-stitching, beading, and appliqué. These finishing details add an element of refinement and ensure that your accessories complement the bride's gown and personal style.

Inspiration and Design Considerations

Creating wedding accessories is not solely about following patterns and instructions; it also involves inspiration and creativity. Draw inspiration from fashion magazines, online galleries, and real-life weddings. Consider the bride's personality, the wedding theme, and the overall style of the event when designing your accessories.

Care and Maintenance

Ensure your wedding accessories remain pristine and beautiful for years to come. Learn the proper care and maintenance techniques for delicate fabrics and embellishments. Understanding how to store, clean, and preserve these items will extend their lifespan and allow you to cherish them as treasured mementos of the special day.

Embark on a creative adventure and discover the joy of crafting exquisite wedding accessories. With the guidance provided in this one, you will gain the skills and knowledge to create unique and beautiful adornments that will enhance the elegance and romance of any bridal celebration.

8.2: Sewing Party Decorations

A sewing party is an opportunity to gather with fellow enthusiasts, share knowledge, and indulge in the joy of crafting. The ambiance plays a pivotal role in setting the tone and creating a memorable experience. Decorations, carefully chosen and thoughtfully arranged, can transform an ordinary gathering into a whimsical and inspiring space.

Floral accents, brimming with vibrant hues and delicate fragrances, bring a touch of nature's charm to the party. Consider using fresh flowers, arranging them in eye-catching vases or adorning the tables with vibrant garlands. Alternatively, artificial flowers, with their durability and versatility, offer a budget-friendly option that can add a splash of color and elegance to the venue.

Fabric swatches, in a kaleidoscope of colors and textures, evoke the essence of sewing. Drape them over tables, use them to create charming bunting, or fashion them into unique wall hangings. The tactile appeal of different fabrics invites guests to explore and imagine the possibilities that lie within their own creative projects.

Lighting, both natural and artificial, sets the mood for the party. Natural light, streaming through windows, creates a bright and airy atmosphere. Artificial lighting, strategically placed, can enhance the ambiance and create focal points. String lights, twinkling with a soft glow, add a touch of whimsy, while table lamps, casting a warm and inviting light, encourage guests to linger and share their sewing adventures.

Personalized touches, such as handmade decorations, reflect the spirit of the occasion. Cross-stitch patterns, featuring sewing-themed designs, can be framed and displayed on walls. Mini quilts, showcasing a variety of stitches and fabrics, can be used as coasters or table centerpieces. The inclusion of these handcrafted elements adds a personal touch and celebrates the creativity of the attendees.

With careful planning and attention to detail, you can create a sewing party decoration scheme that not only complements the occasion but also inspires the creative spirits of your guests. From floral arrangements to fabric displays, from lighting to personalized touches, each element contributes to a cohesive and unforgettable experience. As you gather with fellow sewing enthusiasts, let the ambiance serve as a canvas upon which the joy of creating unfolds.

8.3: Making Gifts for Loved Ones

Crafting personalized gifts for loved ones is an incredibly rewarding experience that can strengthen bonds and express heartfelt emotions. Handmade gifts, imbued with time, effort, and creativity, possess a unique sentimental value that transcends material worth. In this one, we will explore the fundamentals of sewing for special occasions, empowering you to create meaningful and memorable presents for the people you cherish.

Consider the recipient's personality, interests, and lifestyle when selecting a gift idea. Determine their favorite colors, patterns, and fabrics to ensure the gift aligns with their tastes. Personalizing the gift with embroidery, appliqués, or unique embellishments adds an extra touch of thoughtfulness and exclusivity.

Planning the project in advance will help you avoid any last-minute hiccups and ensure a successful outcome.

Choosing the right fabric is crucial for both the aesthetic and functional aspects of the gift. For beginners, opting for lightweight and easy-to-sew fabrics like cotton, linen, or flannel is recommended. Consider the intended purpose of the item; for instance, a durable fabric like canvas or denim would be suitable for a bag or cushion cover, while a soft and cuddly fabric like fleece or velvet would be ideal for a blanket or stuffed animal.

Mastering basic sewing techniques is essential for crafting polished and well-constructed gifts. Practice stitches like the straight stitch, zigzag stitch, and topstitch to achieve neat and secure seams. Familiarize yourself with essential sewing tools and their functions, such as a sewing machine, needles, thread, scissors, and measuring tape. Additionally, learning basic pattern reading skills will allow you to customize your creations and expand your sewing capabilities.

When sewing for special occasions, attention to detail is paramount. Take the time to press seams, ensuring they lie flat and crisp. Consider adding decorative touches like buttons, ribbons, or lace to enhance the gift's visual appeal. Personalize the gift with a heartfelt note or handwritten inscription to make it truly one-of-a-kind and cherished for years to come.

Remember that the most important aspect of making gifts for loved ones is the love and intention you put into them. Whether you choose a simple or elaborate design, the time and effort you dedicate to the project will be evident in the finished product. Embrace the creative process and let your imagination soar as you stitch together a gift that will be treasured for its sentimental value and bring joy to its recipient.

8.4: Designing Unique and Personalized Items

In the realm of sewing, personalization transcends mere embellishments; it's an art form that imbues garments and accessories with a profound sense of individuality. It's not about replicating mass-produced designs but rather about creating one-of-a-kind pieces that reflect the wearer's unique personality, style, and aspirations. Personalized items evoke a sense of exclusivity, allowing individuals to express their creativity and stand out from the crowd.

Embracing the Creative Process

Designing unique and personalized items begins with understanding the client's vision and preferences. Active listening and open communication are crucial to capturing their desires and translating them into tangible creations. The designer should possess a keen eye for detail, an appreciation for different fabrics and textures, and an ability to envision how these elements will come together to create a cohesive and visually appealing masterpiece.

Transforming Ideas into Reality

The creative process unfolds through a series of steps. First, the designer sketches out their ideas, exploring different designs and experimenting with fabric combinations. Once a design is finalized, a pattern is created to guide the sewing process. Fabric selection is of paramount importance, as it can dramatically alter the look and feel of the finished product. Careful consideration should be given to the fabric's weight, texture, drape, and compatibility with the intended design.

Attention to Detail and Precision

Sewing personalized items requires meticulous attention to detail and precision. Each stitch should be executed with care to ensure a professional and polished finish. The use of appropriate sewing techniques and embellishments can elevate the design and make it truly unique. Hand-stitching, for instance, adds an exquisite touch that sets it apart from machine-made items. Embroidered details, lace trim, or intricate beadwork can further enhance the item's appeal.

Collaboration and Feedback

Throughout the design process, collaboration and feedback are essential. The designer should regularly consult with the client to ensure that their vision is being realized. Open communication allows for adjustments and modifications to be made along the way, ensuring that the final product meets the client's expectations. Feedback from the client can also inspire new ideas and contribute to the overall success of the design.

Preserving Sentimental Value

Personalized items often hold immense sentimental value. They may be created to commemorate special occasions, such as weddings, anniversaries, or birthdays. By incorporating personal touches and mementos into the design, the item becomes a cherished keepsake that can be passed down through generations. The act of creating personalized items is not merely about producing a garment or accessory; it's about creating a tangible expression of love, friendship, or celebration.

Chapter 9: Advanced Sewing Techniques

9.1: Working with Zippers

Zippers, ubiquitous in modern garments, offer versatility and convenience. Familiarizing yourself with the various types and their suitability for specific applications is crucial. Common zipper types include coil, invisible, and metal zippers, each with its unique characteristics. Coil zippers, with their spiral teeth, provide flexibility and are ideal for casual clothing and bags. Invisible zippers, as the name suggests, seamlessly blend into the fabric, making them ideal for formal attire or garments where a discreet closure is desired. Metal zippers, constructed with durable interlocking teeth, offer strength and durability, making them suitable for heavy-duty applications such as outdoor gear or luggage.

Mastering Zipper Insertion Techniques:

Inserting zippers into garments requires precision and a systematic approach. Begin by selecting the appropriate zipper length and type for the specific application. Carefully mark the seam line where the zipper will be inserted, ensuring alignment and symmetry. Use the zipper foot on your sewing machine to guide the zipper accurately, ensuring even stitching along its length. For invisible zippers, special techniques are employed to conceal the stitching and create a seamless finish.

Troubleshooting Common Zipper Issues:

Even with careful technique, issues may arise during zipper insertion or use. A common problem is the zipper sticking or jamming. This can be caused by fabric getting caught in the teeth or misaligned zipper halves. Carefully inspect the zipper and remove any obstructions. Realign the zipper halves and apply a lubricant such as graphite or candle wax to smooth the teeth. If the zipper continues to stick, seek professional repair to avoid further damage.

Tips for Achieving Professional Zipper Finishes:

Attention to detail and a few finishing touches can elevate the appearance and functionality of zippers. Topstitch the zipper to secure it and reinforce the seam. Consider using a matching thread or contrasting thread for a decorative effect. Add a zipper pull or tab for ease of use and a touch of personalization. Remember to test the zipper's smoothness and durability before finalizing the garment.

Additional Considerations:

Zippers come in a range of colors and finishes to complement different fabrics and styles. Consider the overall aesthetic of the garment and choose a zipper that blends seamlessly or adds a contrasting accent. For garments exposed to frequent washing, choose zippers made of rust-resistant materials to maintain their integrity over time. With practice and a thorough understanding of zipper types and techniques, you can confidently tackle zipper insertion, ensuring professional-looking finishes in your sewing projects.

9.2: Sewing Buttons and Buttonholes

The type of button you choose will depend on the fabric, the garment, and the desired look. Buttons come in a wide variety of materials, including plastic, metal, wood, shell, and leather. Plastic buttons are lightweight and inexpensive, making them a good choice for everyday garments. Metal buttons are more durable and can add a touch of elegance to a garment. Wood buttons are natural and can give a garment a rustic look. Shell buttons are made from the shells of mollusks and can add a touch of sophistication to a garment. Leather buttons are durable and can add a touch of warmth to a garment.

Measuring and Marking Buttonholes

Before you can sew a buttonhole, you need to measure and mark the location of the buttonhole. The placement of the buttonhole will depend on the type of garment and the desired look. Once you have determined the location of the buttonhole, use a marking pen or chalk to mark the center of the buttonhole.

Sewing Buttonholes

There are a variety of ways to sew buttonholes. The most common method is to use a sewing machine. Buttonholes can also be sewn by hand, but this is a more time-consuming process. If you are using a sewing machine, select a buttonhole stitch. The buttonhole stitch will vary depending on the type of sewing machine you have. Follow the instructions in your sewing machine manual to sew the buttonhole.

Attaching Buttons

Buttons can be attached to a garment by hand or by

machine. If you are attaching buttons by hand, use a needle and thread to sew the buttons through the holes in the garment. If you are attaching buttons by machine, select a buttonhole stitch. The buttonhole stitch will vary depending on the type of sewing machine you have. Follow the instructions in your sewing machine manual to sew the buttons.

Tips for Sewing Buttons and Buttonholes

Use a sharp needle. A dull needle will be more likely to break or damage the fabric.
Use the correct thread. The thread should be strong enough to hold the button in place, but not so strong that it will damage the fabric.
Use a thimble. A thimble will protect your finger from the needle.
Be patient. Sewing buttons and buttonholes can be time-consuming, but it is important to take your time to ensure that the buttons are sewn securely.

9.3: Using Elastics and Cords

There are two main categories of elastics: woven and knitted. Woven elastics are made from interwoven rubber threads and synthetic fibers, resulting in a durable and firm material. They come in various widths and strengths, making them suitable for applications such as waistbands, swimwear, and lingerie. Knitted elastics, on the other hand, are created by knitting rubber yarns, producing a soft and stretchy fabric. They are often used for delicate items like lace trim, smocking, and ruffles.

Cords, available in a range of materials such as cotton, polyester, and nylon, serve diverse purposes in sewing. They can reinforce seams, add decorative accents, or create functional features like drawstrings. Cotton cords, known for their breathability and natural appearance, are commonly used in home décor projects like curtains and pillows. Polyester cords offer durability and resistance to stretching, making them ideal for backpacks, bags, and outdoor gear. Nylon cords, with their exceptional strength and elasticity, are often employed in climbing equipment, pet leashes, and bungee cords.

When selecting elastics and cords for a specific project, consider factors such as the desired stretchiness, durability, and aesthetic appeal. It is essential to choose elastics that are compatible with the fabric and application. For instance, a lightweight knitted elastic may be suitable for delicate fabrics, while a sturdy woven elastic is ideal for heavy-duty garments or upholstery. Cords should be chosen based on their intended use, ensuring they can withstand the expected loads and provide the desired functionality or decorative effect.

The proper application of elastics and cords is crucial for achieving optimal results. Elastics can be sewn on using a zigzag stitch or a specialized elastic stitch on your sewing machine. It is essential to adjust the stitch tension and length to ensure the elastic retains its stretchiness without breaking. Cords can be sewn in place using a straight stitch or a decorative stitch, depending on the desired effect. When sewing with cords, use a needle that is appropriate for the cord's thickness and material to prevent damage to the cord or fabric. Understanding their different types and applications enables sewers to make informed choices and achieve professional-looking results. Whether using elastics for a comfortable waistband or cords for a decorative accent, these materials enhance the creativity and versatility of sewing projects.

9.4: Applying Interfacing and Fusible Web

Interfacing, the unsung hero of the sewing world, is a fabric backing that provides structure, stability, and shape to garments and accessories. It comes in various weights and materials, each designed for specific purposes. Woven interfacing, made from tightly woven fibers, adds firmness and helps prevent stretching.

Fusible interfacing, with its heat-activated adhesive, bonds to fabrics, creating a strong and permanent bond. Non-fusible interfacing, applied with stitches, allows for easy removal or repositioning.

Interfacing plays a crucial role in shaping collars, cuffs, waistbands, and other garment details that require crispness and support. It prevents fabrics from sagging or losing their shape, ensuring a professional and polished finish. Choosing the right interfacing weight and type is essential for achieving the desired effect without adding unnecessary bulk or stiffness.

Fusible Web: The Magic Adhesive for Appliqués and Embellishments

Fusible web, a double-sided adhesive interfacing, allows for quick and easy application of appliqués, patches, and other embellishments onto fabrics. It bonds permanently under the heat of an iron, eliminating the need for sewing. Fusible web comes in various weights, suitable for different types of fabrics and embellishments.

When using fusible web, careful alignment and precise application are crucial to avoid unwanted adhesive residue or shifting. It is essential to test the adhesive strength on a scrap fabric before applying it to the main garment. Fusible web adds a touch of creativity and personalization to sewing projects, making it a versatile tool for embellishing garments, home décor, and accessories.

Combining Interfacing and Fusible Web: The Ultimate Duo

Interfacing and fusible web can be combined to achieve even more complex and sophisticated results. By applying interfacing to the back of the fabric before using fusible web to attach embellishments, you create a solid foundation that prevents stretching or tearing. This technique is particularly useful for delicate fabrics or when applying heavy embellishments that require extra support.

Interfacing and fusible web, when used skillfully, elevate sewing projects by providing structure, support, and adhesive bonding. They enable sewers to create garments and accessories that are not only beautiful but also durable and professionally finished. These essential tools empower sewers to explore their creativity and bring their sewing dreams to life.

9.5: Techniques for Embellishments and Trims

One of the most popular techniques for embellishing fabric is embroidery. Embroidery involves stitching decorative designs onto fabric, and it can be done by hand or by machine. Hand embroidery is a relatively simple technique to learn, and it can be used to create a wide variety of designs. Machine embroidery is more complex, but it can be used to create more intricate designs more quickly.

Another popular technique for embellishing fabric is appliqué. Appliqué involves sewing pieces of fabric onto another piece of fabric. Appliqué can be used to create a wide variety of designs, from simple shapes to complex pictures.

In addition to embroidery and appliqué, there are many other techniques for embellishing fabric, such as beading, sequins, and lace. Beading involves sewing beads onto fabric, and it can be used to create a variety of designs, from simple embellishments to elaborate patterns. Sequins are small, shiny discs that can be sewn onto fabric to create a sparkling effect. Lace is a delicate fabric that can be used to add a touch of elegance to any garment.

Trims are another way to add personality and style to any garment. Trims can be used to finish edges, add decorative details, or simply add a touch of color. There are many different types of trims available, such as ribbon, braid, and fringe.

The best way to learn how to embellish and trim fabric is to practice. Experiment with different techniques and materials until you find the ones that you enjoy the most. With a little practice, you will be able to create beautiful and unique garments that will be sure to turn heads.

Chapter 10: Exploring Different Fabric Types

10.1: Cotton: Properties and Uses

1. Breathability: Cotton's cellular structure allows for air circulation, making it a breathable fabric that keeps wearers comfortable in warm weather. This property is particularly beneficial for summer clothing, bedding, and sportswear.

2. Moisture Absorbency: Cotton is highly absorbent, capable of holding up to 27 times its weight in moisture. This makes it an ideal choice for towels, bathrobes, and other items intended to absorb moisture. Additionally, its absorbency contributes to its breathability, as it wicks away perspiration from the body.

3. Softness: Cotton fibers are soft and smooth, resulting in fabrics that are gentle on the skin. This softness makes cotton suitable for use in clothing items that come into direct contact with the body, such as undergarments, t-shirts, and baby clothes.

4. Durability: Cotton is a durable fiber that can withstand repeated washing and wear. Its strong fibers resist tearing and abrasion, ensuring that cotton garments and other items maintain their integrity over time. This durability makes cotton a cost-effective choice for everyday use.

5. Biodegradability: Cotton is a natural, biodegradable fiber that decomposes over time. This eco-friendly attribute aligns with sustainable practices, reducing the environmental impact of discarded cotton products.

Due to its desirable properties, cotton finds applications in a wide range of products, including:

1. Apparel: Cotton is a staple fiber in the clothing industry, used to produce a vast array of garments, from casual t-shirts and jeans to formal attire. Its breathability, comfort, and durability make it suitable for all types of clothing, including everyday wear, sportswear, and special occasion outfits.

2. Home Textiles: Cotton is extensively used in home textiles, such as bed sheets, towels, curtains, and upholstery. Its moisture absorbency makes it an ideal choice for towels, while its softness and breathability

contribute to comfortable bedding. Cotton curtains provide privacy and light control while adding a touch of elegance to any room.

3. Medical and Healthcare: Cotton's hypoallergenic and absorbent properties make it well-suited for medical and healthcare applications. It is used in bandages, gauze, surgical gowns, and other medical supplies. Its breathability and comfort also make it suitable for hospital gowns and patient clothing.

4. Industrial Uses: Cotton is not limited to consumer products; it also finds uses in industrial applications. Its strength and durability make it a suitable material for canvas, tarpaulins, and other heavy-duty fabrics used in construction, agriculture, and transportation.

5. Personal Care Products: Cotton is used in a variety of personal care products, such as cotton balls, swabs, and facial pads. Its softness and absorbency make it gentle on the skin, ideal for use in these delicate applications.

In summary, cotton's exceptional properties, including breathability, moisture absorbency, softness, durability, and biodegradability, make it a versatile and highly valued fiber in the textile industry. Its wide range of applications, from apparel to home textiles, medical supplies, and industrial uses, demonstrates its adaptability and enduring appeal.

10.2: Silk: Luxurious and Versatile

The versatility of silk extends far beyond its use in exquisite clothing. Its delicate yet robust nature lends itself to a diverse range of applications, from home décor to medical textiles. In the realm of interior design, silk's inherent beauty and drape add a touch of sophistication to curtains, upholstery, and bedding. Its natural insulation properties contribute to a cozy and inviting ambiance, while its ability to regulate temperature ensures year-round comfort.

In the medical field, silk's biocompatibility and antibacterial qualities have made it a valuable material for surgical sutures, wound dressings, and other medical devices. Its ability to promote cell growth and tissue regeneration has led to its use in biomedical engineering and tissue scaffolding. Silk's versatility and therapeutic properties have garnered significant interest in the development of innovative medical applications.

Furthermore, silk's unique structure and properties have sparked scientific research and technological advancements. Its ability to refract light has been harnessed to create iridescent textiles that mimic the colors and patterns found in nature. Advances in nanotechnology have enabled the incorporation of silk into composite materials, enhancing their strength, toughness, and biocompatibility. These innovations continue to push the boundaries of silk's applications, unlocking its potential in fields such as optics, electronics, and renewable energy. From luxurious garments to medical textiles and cutting-edge scientific applications, silk's allure and utility remain unmatched. Its enduring legacy is a testament to the transformative power of natural fibers and the enduring appeal of beauty, comfort, and innovation.

10.3: Wool: Warm and Durable

In addition to its thermal qualities, wool possesses remarkable durability, owing to its strong and resilient fibers. This durability translates into garments that can withstand wear and tear, making them long-lasting and suitable for everyday use. Wool fabrics exhibit resistance to abrasion, making them less prone to pilling and fraying compared to other fibers. Furthermore, the natural elasticity of wool allows garments to retain their shape and structure, ensuring a comfortable fit and a polished appearance.

The versatility of wool extends beyond its practical

qualities. Its unique texture and aesthetic appeal have made it a popular choice for both casual and formal attire. Wool fabrics can be woven into a range of textures, from soft and cozy knits to smooth and polished worsteds. This versatility allows designers to create garments that cater to diverse tastes and styles.

Wool's natural breathability is another key attribute that contributes to its comfort and wearability. Wool fibers allow air to circulate, preventing the buildup of moisture and keeping the wearer dry and comfortable. This breathability makes wool garments suitable for both indoor and outdoor activities, as they can help regulate body temperature and prevent overheating.

However, it is important to note that wool requires proper care and maintenance to preserve its qualities. Regular dry cleaning or hand washing is recommended to prevent shrinkage and maintain the integrity of the fibers. Additionally, wool garments should be stored in a cool, dry place to protect them from moths and other pests that can damage the fabric. Its inherent qualities make it an excellent choice for a wide range of textile applications, from cozy winter garments to stylish and sophisticated attire. With proper care, wool fabrics can provide years of comfort and enjoyment, making them a valuable investment for any wardrobe.

10.4: Linen: Natural and Breathable

The flax plant, from which linen is obtained, is meticulously cultivated for its sturdy fibers. These fibers undergo a labor-intensive process involving retting, breaking, and scutching to extract the valuable linen fibers. The resulting yarns are renowned for their exceptional tensile strength, making linen fabrics highly durable and resistant to wear and tear. This durability ensures that linen garments can withstand repeated washing and wear, maintaining their pristine appearance over time.

In addition to its durability, linen is celebrated for its exceptional moisture-wicking properties. The fibers possess a natural affinity for moisture, drawing it away from the body and allowing it to evaporate quickly. This remarkable ability makes linen an ideal choice for garments intended for warm and humid environments. Linen fabrics keep the wearer cool and comfortable, even during strenuous activities or on sweltering days.

Furthermore, linen is highly breathable, allowing air to circulate freely through its weave. This breathability contributes to the overall comfort of linen garments, as it prevents the buildup of heat and moisture against the skin. The airy nature of linen makes it particularly suitable for summer wear, as it helps regulate body temperature and promotes a sense of well-being.

The luxurious drape of linen is another attribute that sets it apart from other fabrics. Linen fabrics possess a characteristic fluidity and movement that creates a graceful and elegant silhouette. This drape lends itself beautifully to garments such as flowing dresses, skirts, and blouses, where the fabric's soft folds and gentle movement add an air of sophistication and charm.

Linen's exceptional qualities extend beyond its aesthetic appeal. It is also a sustainable choice, as the flax plant requires minimal water and pesticides to grow. Additionally, linen is biodegradable and recyclable, making it an environmentally friendly option for conscious consumers. Its natural origin, moisture-wicking properties, and luxurious drape make it an ideal choice for a wide range of garments, from casual wear to formal attire. Linen's enduring appeal is a testament to its timeless qualities and its ability to elevate any wardrobe with its inherent beauty and sophistication.

10.5: Synthetic Fabrics: Polyester, Nylon, Spandex

Synthetic fabrics, a testament to modern textile technology, have revolutionized the world of clothing and home décor. These man-made fibers, unlike their natural counterparts, are crafted from synthetic polymers, offering a myriad of advantages that make them indispensable in a variety of applications.

Polyester, a pioneer in the synthetic fabric realm, is renowned for its exceptional strength and durability. Its ability to resist fading, shrinking, and wrinkles makes it an ideal choice for garments that endure frequent washing and wear. From wrinkle-resistant dress shirts to outdoor gear that withstands the elements, polyester's versatility knows no bounds.

Nylon, another synthetic stalwart, possesses an impressive combination of strength, elasticity, and resistance to abrasion. This makes it a prime material for sportswear, swimwear, and other activewear garments. Nylon's quick-drying properties and ability to wick moisture away from the body ensure comfort and performance even during strenuous activities.

Spandex, the epitome of elasticity, is a synthetic fiber that stretches to several times its original length without losing its shape. Its unique properties have made it an indispensable component in activewear, sportswear, and medical garments that require flexibility and support. Spandex's ability to conform to the body's movements while providing gentle compression makes it ideal for garments designed to enhance performance and promote recovery.

Advantages of Synthetic Fabrics

The allure of synthetic fabrics stems from their inherent advantages, which make them a compelling choice for a wide range of applications:

Durability: Synthetic fabrics are exceptionally strong and resistant to wear and tear, ensuring longevity even with frequent use.
Wrinkle Resistance: These fabrics are less prone to wrinkling, making them easy to care for and maintain a polished appearance.
Moisture Management: Some synthetic fabrics, like nylon, have moisture-wicking properties, drawing sweat away from the body and keeping the wearer dry and comfortable.
Stain Resistance: Synthetic fibers often have stain-resistant qualities, making them ideal for garments and fabrics that are likely to encounter spills and messes.
Affordability: Compared to natural fibers, synthetic fabrics are often more affordable, making them accessible to a wider range of consumers.

Applications of Synthetic Fabrics

The versatility of synthetic fabrics makes them

suitable for a vast array of applications:

Clothing: Synthetic fabrics are commonly used in everyday clothing, from casual wear to formal attire. Their durability and wrinkle resistance make them ideal for garments that require minimal care.
Activewear: The elasticity and moisture-wicking properties of synthetic fabrics make them a top choice for sportswear and activewear, enhancing performance and comfort.
Home Décor: Synthetic fabrics are often used in curtains, upholstery, and other home décor items, offering a range of textures, colors, and patterns.
Medical Textiles: The elasticity and moisture-wicking properties of synthetic fabrics make them suitable for medical garments such as compression bandages and surgical gowns.

Choosing the Right Synthetic Fabric

Selecting the appropriate synthetic fabric for a specific application requires careful consideration of its unique characteristics:

Polyester: Known for its strength, durability, and wrinkle resistance, polyester is a versatile choice for clothing, home décor, and industrial applications.
Nylon: With its combination of strength, elasticity, and

moisture-wicking properties, nylon excels in activewear, swimwear, and other applications that demand both durability and flexibility.

Spandex: The epitome of elasticity, spandex is indispensable in garments that require exceptional flexibility, such as activewear, sportswear, and medical textiles.

Synthetic fabrics have become an integral part of our modern world, offering a remarkable blend of durability, versatility, and affordability. From the ruggedness of polyester to the elasticity of spandex, these man-made fibers have revolutionized the way we clothe ourselves, decorate our homes, and support our well-being. As technology continues to advance, the possibilities for synthetic fabrics are boundless, promising even greater innovation and applications in the years to come.

Chapter 11: Embroidery and Decorative Stitches

11.1: Hand Embroidery Basics

Embroidery begins with selecting the appropriate fabric and thread. Natural fibers like cotton, linen, and silk provide a stable base for embroidery, while the choice of thread depends on the desired effect. Cotton thread is durable and versatile, while silk thread adds a touch of elegance and sheen.

The fundamental stitch in hand embroidery is the running stitch. This basic stitch creates a continuous line of evenly spaced stitches, forming the foundation for more complex patterns. The back stitch, a variation of the running stitch, provides a stronger and more secure line.

Beyond these essential stitches, a wide range of decorative stitches enhance the visual appeal of embroidery. The satin stitch, with its smooth, lustrous surface, is ideal for filling in shapes and creating bold accents. The French knot, a small, raised knot, adds texture and dimension to designs. The lazy daisy stitch, resembling a blooming flower, brings a whimsical touch to embroidery.

Embroidery techniques extend beyond individual stitches to encompass various approaches. Needle painting, akin to painting with a needle and thread, uses a range of stitches to create realistic and detailed images. Appliqué, the art of attaching fabric pieces to a base fabric, adds a unique dimension to embroidery designs.

Embroidery not only beautifies fabrics but also carries cultural significance. Traditional embroidery patterns often reflect regional heritage and folklore, preserving centuries-old stories and traditions. In contemporary embroidery, artists push the boundaries of the craft, incorporating innovative materials and techniques to create modern masterpieces.

Whether pursuing embroidery for its artistic merits, cultural significance, or simply as a relaxing hobby, this versatile craft offers endless opportunities for creativity and self-expression. With patience, practice, and a touch of inspiration, anyone can master the basics of hand embroidery and embark on a journey of artistic exploration.

11.2: Common Embroidery Stitches

Embroidery, a craft adorned with centuries of tradition, offers a captivating realm of needle and thread. From the intricate motifs of the Orient to the bold patterns of Scandinavian folk art, embroidery stitches have adorned garments, tapestries, and decorative objects throughout history. This one embarks on an exploration of the most commonly encountered embroidery stitches, providing a comprehensive guide for both novice and seasoned stitchers alike.

The art of embroidery encompasses a vast repertoire of stitches, each possessing its unique character and versatility. Some stitches, such as the running stitch, are fundamental building blocks, serving as the foundation for more complex designs. Others, like the French knot, lend a touch of elegance and dimension, while stitches such as the bullion knot add a sculptural element to embroidered creations.

Embroidery threads, available in an array of materials, colors, and weights, play a pivotal role in defining the final outcome. Silk threads, renowned for their luxurious sheen and durability, are often employed in traditional embroidery techniques. Cotton threads, versatile and affordable, offer a wide range of colors and are suitable for a variety of projects. Metallic threads, shimmering with a touch of glamour, add a touch of brilliance to special occasions.

Whether embarking on a simple project or a grand tapestry, understanding the basics of embroidery stitches is essential. This one provides a thorough examination of these fundamental stitches, guiding readers through their steps, variations, and applications.

Running Stitch: The Embroiderer's Foundation

The running stitch, the cornerstone of embroidery, forms the basis for countless other stitches. Its simple yet effective nature makes it suitable for both beginners and experienced stitchers alike. As the needle weaves in and out of the fabric, a continuous line is created, forming the outline of shapes and motifs. The running stitch can be varied in length and spacing, allowing for customization and the creation of a wide range of effects.

Backstitch: Precision and Stability

The backstitch, a robust and versatile stitch, provides stability and definition to embroidered designs. It is often used for outlines, lettering, and areas that require a secure hold. The backstitch creates a series of small, even stitches that interlock, forming a solid line.

This stitch is particularly effective for fine details and intricate patterns, ensuring that the design remains crisp and clear.

Stem Stitch: Creating Delicate Lines

The stem stitch, a popular choice for outlining and filling, mimics the appearance of a plant stem. Its slanted stitches create a continuous line that can be varied in width and density. The stem stitch is ideal for creating flowing curves and delicate details, adding a touch of elegance to embroidered designs. Its versatility makes it suitable for both contemporary and traditional embroidery styles.

French Knot: A Touch of Dimension

The French knot, an alluring stitch that adds a touch of dimension and texture, is a staple in embroidery. Its small, raised knots resemble miniature flowers or beads, creating a captivating effect. Mastering the French knot requires practice and patience, but once perfected, it opens up a world of creative possibilities. This stitch is often used to accentuate flowers, leaves, and other intricate motifs, adding a touch of charm and sophistication.

Bullion Knot: Sculptural Elements

The bullion knot, a three-dimensional stitch, elevates embroidery to a new level. Its twisted loops create a sculptural element, adding depth and texture to designs. The bullion knot requires a bit more dexterity, but its striking appearance makes it well worth the effort. This stitch is often used to create flowers, vines, and other decorative elements, bringing a sense of movement and vitality to embroidered creations.

11.3: Machine Embroidery Techniques

Embroidery is the art of embellishing fabric or other materials with decorative stitches using a needle and thread. Machine embroidery is a type of embroidery that uses a sewing machine to create the stitches. Machine embroidery can be used to create a wide variety of designs, from simple outlines to complex and colorful patterns.

There are two main types of machine embroidery: free-motion embroidery and computerized embroidery. Free-motion embroidery is done by guiding the fabric under the needle by hand, while computerized embroidery is done by programming a sewing machine to follow a specific design.

Free-motion embroidery is a great way to add a

personal touch to your sewing projects. It is a relatively simple technique to learn, and it can be used to create a wide variety of designs. Computerized embroidery is a more advanced technique, but it allows you to create very precise and intricate designs.

Free-Motion Embroidery

Free-motion embroidery is a type of embroidery that is done by guiding the fabric under the needle by hand. This gives you a lot of freedom to create unique and expressive designs. Free-motion embroidery can be used to create a wide variety of designs, from simple outlines to complex and colorful patterns.

To do free-motion embroidery, you will need a sewing machine with a free-motion foot. A free-motion foot is a special type of presser foot that allows the fabric to move freely under the needle. You will also need a variety of embroidery threads and needles.

To start free-motion embroidery, thread your machine with the desired thread and needle. Then, set your machine to the free-motion setting. This setting will allow you to move the fabric under the needle by hand.

To create a design, simply guide the fabric under the needle and stitch. You can use a variety of stitches to create different effects. For example, you can use a straight stitch to create outlines, a zigzag stitch to create texture, or a satin stitch to create a smooth, shiny surface.

Computerized Embroidery

Computerized embroidery is a type of embroidery that is done by programming a sewing machine to follow a specific design. This allows you to create very precise and intricate designs. Computerized embroidery is a great option for creating logos, monograms, and other detailed designs.

To do computerized embroidery, you will need a sewing machine with a computerized embroidery module. A computerized embroidery module is a special attachment that allows you to program the machine to follow a specific design. You will also need a computer and embroidery software.

To create a design for computerized embroidery, you can use a variety of software programs. There are many different software programs available, so you can choose one that fits your needs and budget. Once you have created a design, you can transfer it to your sewing machine using a USB cable or a memory card.

To start computerized embroidery, thread your machine with the desired thread and needle. Then, load the design into the machine and start stitching. The machine will follow the design and create the stitches automatically.

11.4: Adding Embroidered Details to Projects

Embroidered details can enhance the beauty and functionality of various projects, from clothing and home décor to accessories and gifts. Whether you're a seasoned sewist or just starting your embroidery journey, this guide provides a comprehensive overview to help you master this versatile craft.

One of the first steps in embroidery is choosing the right materials. Fabric selection is crucial, as different fabrics have varying textures and weights that can affect the outcome of your embroidery. Similarly, the choice of thread is equally important, with different types of threads offering unique qualities and effects. From cotton and silk to metallic and rayon, the choice of thread can dramatically alter the look and feel of your embroidered details.

Embroidery techniques are as diverse as the designs themselves. From classic hand embroidery stitches like satin stitch, chain stitch, and running stitch, to more elaborate and intricate machine embroidery designs, the options are endless. Each stitch creates a distinct texture and effect, allowing you to customize your embroidery to suit your personal style.

Understanding the basics of embroidery is essential before embarking on your creative journey. The tension of your stitches, the direction of your stitches, and the use of proper tools and equipment all play a significant role in achieving beautiful and long-lasting embroidery results. Practice and patience are key, as mastering the art of embroidery requires time and dedication.

As you gain proficiency in embroidery, you can begin exploring more advanced techniques. Appliqué, for instance, involves attaching fabric shapes or motifs onto a base fabric to create textured and layered effects. Similarly, beading and other embellishments can add an extra dimension to your embroidery, creating visually stunning and tactile pieces.

Embroidery is not merely about replicating designs but also about expressing your creativity and individuality. Experiment with different stitch combinations, thread colors, and embellishments to develop your unique embroidery style. The possibilities are endless, and the only limit is your imagination.

Whether you're looking to personalize a simple tote bag, add intricate details to a special occasion dress, or create unique home décor items, embroidery is a versatile craft that empowers you to transform ordinary projects into extraordinary works of art. Embrace the joy of embroidery and discover the limitless possibilities it offers for self-expression and creative fulfillment.

Chapter 12: Patchwork and Quilting

12.1: Introduction to Patchwork

The basic principles of patchwork are simple. First, choose the fabrics you want to use and cut them into small pieces. The size and shape of the pieces will depend on the desired design. Once the pieces are cut, they are sewn together using a variety of stitches. The most common stitch used for patchwork is the whip stitch, which is a simple and secure stitch that creates a strong bond between the fabric pieces.

There are many different types of patchwork designs, each with its own unique look and feel. Some of the most popular patchwork designs include:

Log cabin: This design is made by sewing together strips of fabric in a log cabin shape.
Nine patch: This design is made by sewing together nine squares of fabric in a 3x3 grid.
Checkerboard: This design is made by sewing together squares of two different colors in a checkerboard

pattern.

Flying geese: This design is made by sewing together two triangles of fabric to form a flying goose shape.

Dresden plate: This design is made by sewing together a circle of fabric with a series of pointed petals.

Patchwork can be used to create a variety of different items, including:

Quilts: Quilts are a traditional form of bedding that is made by sewing together layers of fabric. Patchwork quilts are made by sewing together small pieces of fabric to create a larger, more decorative quilt.

Clothing: Patchwork can be used to create a variety of different clothing items, such as skirts, dresses, and shirts. Patchwork clothing is often unique and stylish, and it can be a great way to add a personal touch to your wardrobe.

Home décor: Patchwork can also be used to create a variety of home décor items, such as pillows, curtains, and tablecloths. Patchwork home décor is a great way to add a touch of color and personality to your home.

Patchwork is a versatile and creative art form that can be used to create a wide variety of items. With a little bit of practice, you can learn the basic principles of patchwork and start creating your own unique and beautiful pieces.

12.2: Basic Patchwork Techniques

Patchwork, a centuries-old craft, involves assembling fabric pieces to create visually captivating designs. In its simplest form, patchwork combines small fabric squares or shapes into a larger fabric piece, often used for quilts, blankets, and home décor. This one delves into the fundamental techniques of patchwork, providing a comprehensive guide for beginners to master the art of creating unique and intricate fabric masterpieces.

The versatility of patchwork lies in its accessibility to sewers of all skill levels. With a few basic tools and techniques, anyone can create stunning patchwork projects. This one introduces the essential tools for patchwork, including rotary cutters, rulers, and cutting mats, and guides readers through the fundamental cutting techniques used to create precise fabric pieces.

Seaming, the process of joining fabric pieces, is a crucial aspect of patchwork. This one explores various seaming methods, such as plain seaming, French seams, and mitered corners, each designed to achieve specific aesthetic and functional results. Readers will gain an understanding of seam allowances, seam finishes, and pressing techniques, enabling them to create durable and professionally finished patchwork projects.

Patchwork often involves piecing together fabric shapes to form intricate patterns. This one introduces the concept of pattern templates, which serve as guides for cutting and assembling fabric pieces. Readers will learn how to create and use pattern templates to create a wide range of patchwork designs, from traditional blocks to modern geometric shapes.

Appliqué, a technique that involves attaching fabric pieces to a background fabric, adds an extra layer of embellishment to patchwork projects. This one covers the different methods of appliqué, such as hand appliqué and machine appliqué, providing step-by-step instructions for each technique. Readers will learn how to choose and prepare fabrics for appliqué, as well as how to create smooth, secure, and visually appealing appliqué designs.

The final section of this one focuses on assembling patchwork blocks into a cohesive quilt top. Readers will learn about different quilt layouts and construction methods, including joining blocks using seams or setting them with sashing or borders. The one concludes with a discussion of quilting techniques, such as hand quilting and machine quilting, which add texture, warmth, and durability to patchwork quilts.

12.3: Quilting Basics: Layers and Batting

In the realm of quilting, layers and batting form the very essence of the craft, providing the structure, warmth, and texture that define a quilt. Understanding these fundamental components is crucial for any aspiring quilter.

The quilt top, the most visible layer, serves as the canvas for the quilter's artistry. It is typically composed of numerous fabric patches sewn together in a myriad of intricate patterns, showcasing the quilter's skill and imagination. The beauty of the quilt top lies in its ability to transform ordinary fabrics into extraordinary works of art.

Beneath the quilt top lies the batting, a layer that provides warmth, insulation, and loft to the quilt. Various types of batting, such as cotton, wool, or polyester, offer different levels of insulation and thickness. The choice of batting depends on the intended use of the quilt and the desired level of warmth.

To draw to a close, the quilt backing forms the

underside of the quilt, providing stability and durability. Typically made from a single piece of fabric, the quilt backing complements the design of the quilt top and ensures that the quilt holds its shape over time.

The careful selection and combination of these layers are essential for creating a quilt that not only meets aesthetic criteria but also fulfills its functional purpose. By mastering the art of layering and batting, quilters can transform fabrics into cherished heirlooms that provide comfort, warmth, and a touch of artistry to any home.

12.4: Creating a Simple Quilt Block

Quilting, an art form with a rich history, involves stitching together pieces of fabric to create intricate and visually stunning designs. At its core, quilting entails creating individual quilt blocks, which are then assembled to form a larger quilt. Understanding the process of constructing a simple quilt block is essential for aspiring quilters.

Step-by-Step Guide to Creating a Simple Quilt Block

Creating a simple quilt block involves a series of precise steps that ensure accuracy and consistency throughout the quilting process. These steps include:

- Selecting Fabric: The choice of fabric for your quilt block is crucial, as it will determine the overall appearance and durability of the final product. Consider the texture, weight, and pattern of the fabric, and ensure it complements the intended design.

- Cutting the Fabric: Using a rotary cutter and a quilting ruler, accurately cut the fabric into the desired shape and size for your quilt block. Precision cutting ensures that the pieces fit together seamlessly, minimizing gaps and irregularities.

- Piecing the Fabric: Join the fabric pieces together using a sewing machine or by hand. Employ a consistent seam allowance to ensure uniformity and a professional finish.

- Pressing the Seams: After piecing, it is essential to press the seams open. This flattens the seams, reduces bulk, and improves the overall appearance of the quilt block.

- Trimming the Excess Fabric: Once the seams are pressed, trim any excess fabric around the edges of the quilt block. This ensures a clean and polished finish.

Exploring Different Quilt Block Patterns

The beauty of quilting lies in its versatility, with countless quilt block patterns available. Each pattern offers a unique design element, contributing to the overall aesthetic of the quilt. Some popular quilt block patterns include:

- Nine-Patch: A classic quilt block featuring nine squares arranged in a 3x3 grid.
- Log Cabin: A traditional quilt block that resembles a log cabin, with strips of fabric arranged in a square or rectangle.
- Flying Geese: A dynamic quilt block that incorporates triangles to create a sense of movement and interest.
- Star: A versatile quilt block that can be made with various sizes and shapes of fabric to create a variety of star designs.
- Drunkard's Path: A curved quilt block that adds a touch of whimsy and complexity to the quilt design.

Mastering the art of creating a simple quilt block is the foundation for successful quilting endeavors. By understanding the essential steps involved and exploring the diverse range of quilt block patterns, aspiring quilters can embark on a rewarding journey of creativity and craftsmanship. Whether for personal enjoyment or as thoughtful gifts, quilts bring beauty, warmth, and a touch of handmade charm to any space.

12.5: Designing and Assembling Quilts

Once the fabric selection is finalized, it's time to determine the quilt's layout. This involves deciding on the size and shape of the quilt, as well as the placement of individual quilt blocks. It's helpful to sketch out the design on paper or use a quilt design software to visualize the layout and ensure balance and symmetry.

The next step is cutting the fabric pieces accurately. Using a sharp rotary cutter and ruler ensures precise cuts, reducing errors during the assembly process. It's essential to pay attention to the grain line of the fabric, which determines the direction of the fabric's drape and strength.

Assembling the quilt blocks is a critical stage that requires patience and attention to detail. Each block is typically made up of smaller fabric pieces sewn together in a specific pattern. Accurate piecing is essential to ensure the quilt blocks fit together seamlessly. It's helpful to use a sewing machine with a walking foot, which helps feed the fabric evenly and prevents puckering.

Once the quilt blocks are assembled, it's time to join them together to form the quilt top. This involves sewing the blocks together in rows, then joining the rows to create the overall quilt top. It's important to use a consistent seam allowance throughout the process to ensure the quilt top is square and lies flat.

The final step is quilting, which involves stitching through the quilt top, batting, and backing fabric layers to secure them together. Quilting can be done by hand or machine, and there are numerous quilting patterns to choose from. The quilting stitches not only add visual interest to the quilt but also provide additional warmth and durability.

When quilting by hand, it's important to use a sharp needle and thread that matches the fabric weight. Hand quilting can be a relaxing and meditative process, allowing for greater control over the stitch length and spacing.

Machine quilting, on the other hand, offers efficiency and precision. Different quilting feet and attachments can be used to create a variety of quilting patterns, from simple straight lines to intricate designs. It's important to practice on scrap fabric before quilting the actual quilt top to ensure the desired results.

Quilt binding is the finishing touch that gives the quilt a polished and professional look. It involves attaching a strip of fabric around the edges of the quilt to enclose the raw edges and provide durability. The binding can be sewn by hand or machine, and it's important to miter the corners neatly for a clean finish.

With careful planning, precision cutting, and meticulous assembly, it's possible to create stunning quilts that showcase personal style and craftsmanship. Whether for warmth, decoration, or as a cherished heirloom, quilts can bring beauty and comfort to any home.

Chapter 13: Sewing for Creativity

13.1: Turning Sewing into a Hobby

As you embark on this creative odyssey, it's essential to nurture your imagination and embrace a playful approach. Allow yourself to experiment with different fabrics, textures, and colors, casting aside any preconceived notions or limitations. Dare to combine unexpected materials and techniques, fostering a spirit of innovation and originality. The beauty of sewing for creativity lies in its liberating nature, where there are no rules or boundaries to stifle your artistic expression.

Moreover, sewing for creativity provides a sanctuary for mindfulness and tranquility. The rhythmic movements of the needle and thread can induce a state of flow, where time seems to dissolve and your focus becomes laser-sharp. The repetitive nature of sewing can have a meditative effect, calming the mind and promoting inner peace. As you immerse yourself in the creative process, worries and distractions melt away, allowing you to fully engage with the present moment and revel in the joy of creating.

As you progress on your creative sewing journey, don't be afraid to seek inspiration from diverse sources. Delve into art books, browse through online galleries, and attend workshops or classes to ignite your imagination and expand your technical skills. Engage with fellow sewers, exchange ideas, and learn from their experiences. The sewing community is a vibrant and supportive network, eager to share knowledge and provide encouragement along the way. Embrace the collective wisdom and creativity that surrounds you, and allow it to fuel your own artistic growth.

To sum up, remember that sewing for creativity is a journey without a predefined destination. It's an ongoing process of exploration, experimentation, and self-discovery. Don't compare your progress to others, but rather focus on your own unique path and the joy of creating. Savor each stitch, each seam, and each finished project as a testament to your creativity and artistic spirit. As you continue to sew for creativity, you will undoubtedly encounter moments of triumph and moments of frustration. Embrace both experiences with equal measure, as they are integral parts of the creative process. Learn from your mistakes, refine your techniques, and never cease to challenge yourself.

13.2: Creative Projects and Upcycling

Sewing, once perceived as a purely functional pursuit, has blossomed into a boundless realm of creativity and artistic expression. In the realm of creative sewing, the traditional notions of purpose and utility have been gracefully surpassed, giving rise to innovative projects and the art of upcycling.

Upcycling, the ingenious process of transforming discarded or unwanted materials into novel and desirable creations, has taken root within the sewing community. This eco-conscious practice not only reduces environmental waste but also breathes new life into overlooked items. From repurposing old fabrics and textiles to reimagining furniture and accessories, upcycling empowers sewers to contribute to a more sustainable and imaginative world.

The boundaries of creative sewing extend far beyond the realm of upcycling. Sewers are now free to explore their artistic sensibilities, experimenting with unconventional materials and techniques. The marriage of sewing with other art forms, such as painting, collage, and embroidery, has resulted in a kaleidoscope of possibilities. Sewing machines have evolved into versatile tools, enabling sewers to create three-dimensional sculptures, intricate textile installations, and wearable art that transcends the realm of mere clothing.

The creative sewing movement has fostered a vibrant and supportive community of makers, designers, and enthusiasts. Online platforms and workshops have become havens for sharing inspiration, exchanging ideas, and showcasing the boundless potential of this craft. Through collaborations and collective projects, creative sewers are pushing the boundaries of their art, fostering a sense of collective creativity that empowers and inspires.

Embarking on a creative sewing journey requires a blend of technical proficiency and an open mind. Beginners may find solace in starting with smaller projects, gradually expanding their skills and experimenting with different materials and techniques. Seeking guidance from experienced sewers, online resources, and workshops can provide invaluable support and inspiration.

As one delves deeper into the world of creative sewing, the possibilities become limitless. The craft transcends the confines of traditional sewing patterns, embracing experimentation and personal expression. Sewers are empowered to create unique and meaningful pieces that reflect their individuality and artistic vision. Whether it's upcycling discarded fabrics into vibrant quilts, transforming old clothes into wearable works of art, or crafting intricate textile sculptures, creative sewing empowers individuals to transform their passion into tangible and expressive creations.

13.3: Exploring Different Sewing Styles

Sewing, an art form that transcends mere fabric manipulation, encompasses a vast array of styles, each imbued with its own distinctive aesthetic and purpose. These styles, influenced by cultural heritage, geographical location, and personal preferences, serve as a testament to the boundless creativity inherent in the craft. Exploring different sewing styles not only enhances technical proficiency but also expands the creative horizons, enabling sewers to express their individuality through their creations.

Deconstructing the Tapestry of Sewing Styles

Embarking on a journey through the tapestry of sewing styles reveals a kaleidoscope of techniques and materials. From the meticulous precision of couture to the vibrant expressiveness of folk embroidery, each style bears a unique story. Understanding the nuances of these styles empowers sewers with the knowledge to choose the most appropriate approach for their projects, ensuring both aesthetic harmony and functional excellence.

Embracing the Timeless Elegance of Couture

Couture, the pinnacle of sewing artistry, epitomizes meticulous attention to detail and impeccable craftsmanship. Rooted in the world of haute couture, this style demands unwavering precision and a mastery of complex techniques. Couturiers, akin to architects of fabric, drape and manipulate materials with surgical precision, creating garments that are both works of art and objects of desire.

Exploring the Vibrant Realm of Folk Embroidery

Folk embroidery, a vibrant tapestry woven from cultural traditions, transports sewers to the heart of diverse communities. Embroidered motifs, stitched with colorful threads, narrate stories, preserve cultural heritage, and adorn garments with an air of authenticity. From the intricate patterns of Ukrainian pysanky to the vibrant hues of Mexican tenangos, folk embroidery celebrates the richness and diversity of human expression.

Discovering the Eclectic Charm of Boho Chic

Boho chic, a bohemian tapestry of eclectic influences,

embraces individuality and free-spirited creativity. This style seamlessly blends elements from different cultures and eras, creating garments that are both stylish and unconventional. Flowing silhouettes, intricate beadwork, and colorful embellishments characterize boho chic, inviting sewers to unleash their imagination and embrace a touch of wanderlust.

Unveiling the Minimalist Serenity of Scandinavian Style

Scandinavian style, renowned for its simplicity and functionality, epitomizes the art of "less is more. " Clean lines, neutral tones, and natural materials define this aesthetic, creating garments that exude effortless elegance and timeless appeal. Scandinavian sewers strive for balance, harmony, and a connection to nature, resulting in pieces that are both aesthetically pleasing and highly wearable.

Navigating the Nuances of Historical Costuming

Historical costuming, a journey through time, transports sewers to different eras and cultures. This style demands meticulous research and attention to detail, as sewers recreate garments from specific historical periods. From the opulent gowns of the Victorian era to the intricate armor of medieval knights, historical costuming offers a unique opportunity to delve into the past and bring its stories to life.

Empowering Sewers with a Creative Compass

Exploring different sewing styles is not merely an exercise in aesthetics but a profound journey of self-discovery. Through this exploration, sewers develop a deeper understanding of their own creative inclinations and preferences. This knowledge empowers them to make informed decisions, experiment with new techniques, and create garments that are truly unique and reflective of their personal style.

13.4: Using Sewing for Self-Expression

Sewing transcends its utilitarian purpose, emerging as a vibrant medium for self-expression. The act of stitching fabric together becomes an extension of one's creativity, allowing individuals to articulate their unique identities and perspectives. Through the choice of materials, color combinations, and design elements, sewers can infuse their creations with personal narratives, emotions, and aspirations.

The diversity of sewing techniques and materials enables individuals to explore a vast spectrum of artistic possibilities. From vibrant textiles to intricate embellishments, each element contributes to the visual language of the final product. By incorporating personal touches and experimental approaches, sewers can transform ordinary garments and accessories into canvases for their own unique artistic visions.

Self-Expression through Creative Projects

The creative potential of sewing extends beyond traditional garments. Sewers can embark on a wide range of projects that serve as outlets for self-expression. Embroidered wall hangings, quilted tapestries, and personalized home decor items offer opportunities to showcase artistic abilities and create meaningful pieces that reflect one's personal style.

The ability to customize and personalize projects allows sewers to create items that resonate deeply with their own experiences and emotions. Whether it's a quilt adorned with cherished family photos or a handmade dress inspired by a favorite painting, sewing empowers individuals to express themselves in tangible and meaningful ways.

Therapeutic Benefits of Creative Sewing

Beyond its artistic merits, sewing also offers

therapeutic benefits that contribute to personal well-being. The rhythmic nature of stitching, the focus on detail, and the satisfaction of completing a project can provide a sense of calm and accomplishment. Engaging in creative sewing activities has been shown to reduce stress levels, improve mood, and enhance feelings of self-esteem.

By providing a platform for self-expression, sewing fosters a sense of personal growth and empowerment. It encourages individuals to embrace their creativity, develop their skills, and find joy in the process of making something unique and meaningful.

Chapter 14: Troubleshooting and Repairs

14.1: Common Sewing Machine Problems

Thread tension problems manifest in uneven stitches, skipped stitches, or puckering of the fabric. Incorrect thread tension can be caused by a variety of factors, including improperly threaded tension discs, worn or damaged tension springs, or a misaligned thread path. Resolving these issues often involves adjusting the tension dial, replacing faulty components, or ensuring the thread passes smoothly through the machine.

Bobbin Problems

Bobbin-related issues commonly result in skipped stitches, loose stitches, or thread tangles. These problems can stem from an improperly wound bobbin, a faulty bobbin case, or a buildup of lint or thread in the bobbin area. To address these issues, it is crucial to ensure proper bobbin winding, clean the bobbin case, and regularly remove any accumulated lint or thread.

Needle Problems

Needle-related problems can manifest in broken needles, skipped stitches, or uneven stitches. These issues often arise due to using the wrong needle type or size for the fabric being sewn, improper needle insertion, or a dull or damaged needle. Resolving these problems involves selecting the appropriate needle, inserting it correctly, and replacing any worn or damaged needles.

Fabric Feed Issues

Fabric feed issues can lead to puckering, uneven stitching, or fabric jamming. These problems can be caused by improper presser foot pressure, worn or damaged feed dogs, or a buildup of lint or thread in the feed area. To address these issues, adjust the presser foot pressure, clean or replace worn feed dogs, and regularly remove any accumulated lint or thread.

Timing Issues

Timing issues can manifest in skipped stitches, broken needles, or uneven stitches. These problems arise when the timing between the needle and hook is incorrect. Resolving timing issues requires professional maintenance or repair, as it involves adjusting the timing mechanism and ensuring proper alignment between the needle and hook.

Electrical Issues

Electrical issues can range from the machine failing to turn on to intermittent power fluctuations. These problems can be caused by loose connections, faulty wiring, or damaged electrical components. Resolving electrical issues often involves checking connections, replacing faulty wires or components, or seeking professional repair.

14.2: Fixing Torn Seams and Holes

Holes in fabrics present a different set of challenges, as they require patching or darning to restore the fabric's integrity. The size and location of the hole will dictate the appropriate repair technique. Smaller holes can be mended using patches, which involve stitching a piece of fabric over the hole to conceal and reinforce the damaged area. Larger holes may necessitate darning, a technique that involves interlacing threads over the hole to create a durable and aesthetically pleasing repair. The choice of thread and fabric for patching or darning should complement the original fabric to ensure a cohesive appearance and maintain the garment's original texture and drape.

When mending holes or tears in delicate fabrics, such as silk or lace, it is crucial to exercise caution to avoid further damage. Hand-stitching techniques, using fine thread and a delicate touch, are often preferred for such fabrics. Additionally, the use of a thimble can protect fingers while providing stability during the stitching process. For more intricate repairs, invisible mending techniques can be employed to minimize the visibility of the repair and maintain the fabric's original appearance. These techniques involve carefully matching the thread color to the fabric and using specialized stitches to blend the repair seamlessly with the surrounding fabric.

Regardless of the repair technique chosen, it is essential to prepare the fabric adequately before proceeding with the mending process. This includes cleaning the fabric to remove any dirt or debris, pressing the fabric to flatten any wrinkles or creases, and stabilizing the torn edges to prevent further fraying. Additionally, using the appropriate tools and materials for the specific fabric type and repair technique will ensure a successful and durable repair. With careful attention to detail and a touch of patience, torn seams and holes can be effectively mended, restoring garments and fabrics to their former glory.

14.3: Repairing Zippers and Buttons

Zippers, while convenient, can be frustrating when they malfunction. However, with a few simple tools and techniques, you can easily repair most zipper issues yourself.

Stuck Zippers: Apply a lubricant, such as graphite or beeswax, to the teeth and slider. Gently work the slider back and forth to distribute the lubricant. If the slider is still stuck, try using a small pair of pliers to gently pull it up or down.

Broken Teeth: If a few teeth are broken, you can replace them with a zipper repair kit. Simply insert the new teeth into the missing slots and use a pair of pliers to crimp them in place.

Slider Replacement: If the slider is damaged or lost, you can easily replace it with a new one. Remove the old slider by unzipping the zipper as far as it will go, then gently pulling the slider off the teeth. Insert the new slider onto the teeth and zip it back up.

Button Repairs

Buttons are another essential component of many garments. While they are typically durable, they can occasionally become loose or fall off. Here's how to repair them:

Loose Buttons: Reattach a loose button by sewing it back on securely with a needle and thread. Use a strong thread that matches the color of the button and make sure to stitch through all layers of the fabric.

Missing Buttons: If a button is missing, you can replace it with a similar one from a sewing kit. Match the size and shape of the button to the original as closely as possible. Sew the new button on using the same technique described above.

Broken Buttons: If a button is broken, it's best to replace it completely. Use a sharp pair of scissors to carefully cut away the old button and replace it with a new one following the steps outlined above.

By following these simple tips, you can easily repair zippers and buttons, extending the life of your garments and preventing minor wardrobe malfunctions.

14.4: Troubleshooting Fabric Issues

Understanding and addressing fabric issues is crucial for achieving successful sewing projects. Common problems include puckering, stretching, and uneven feeding, which can stem from various causes such as fabric type, thread tension, or improper needle selection.

Puckering occurs when the fabric gathers or wrinkles after sewing. This is often caused by using a needle that is too fine or light for the fabric weight, causing the thread to pull the fabric tightly. Additionally, puckering can result from overstretching the fabric during sewing or pressing, which disrupts the natural weave.

Stretching, another common fabric issue, manifests as the fabric elongating excessively during sewing. This is typically caused by using a stitch that is too long or a thread that is too stretchy for the fabric. Excessive stretching can compromise the garment's shape and durability.

Uneven feeding, where the fabric moves through the sewing machine unevenly, can lead to distorted seams and puckering. This issue can be caused by misaligned feed dogs or tension disks, which prevent the fabric from being transported smoothly through the machine.

Worn or damaged feed dogs can also contribute to uneven feeding.

Solutions for Common Fabric Issues:

To resolve fabric puckering, it is essential to select the appropriate needle size and type for the fabric weight and density. Using a heavier needle or one with a larger eye can prevent excessive thread tension. Additionally, avoiding overstretching the fabric during sewing and pressing helps maintain the fabric's natural structure.

Addressing fabric stretching involves adjusting the stitch length and thread choice. Using a shorter stitch length increases the number of stitches per inch, preventing excessive fabric elongation. Opting for a less stretchy thread, such as polyester or cotton, also helps control stretching.

To rectify uneven feeding, it is crucial to ensure the feed dogs are properly aligned and adjusted. If the feed dogs are misaligned, they should be recalibrated according to the sewing machine's instructions. Worn or damaged feed dogs should be replaced promptly to prevent further feeding issues.

Tips for Preventing Fabric Issues:

Preventing fabric issues during sewing begins with selecting the right fabric for the intended purpose and garment design. Understanding the different fabric types and their properties is essential to choosing the most suitable option for the project.

Pre-washing the fabric before sewing removes any sizing or starch that could interfere with the fabric's natural behavior. This step helps prevent shrinkage or puckering after garment construction.

Ironing the fabric before sewing not only prepares the fabric for cutting and sewing but also helps remove wrinkles and creases. A well-pressed fabric feeds smoothly through the sewing machine, minimizing the risk of uneven feeding.

By addressing common fabric issues effectively and taking preventative measures, sewists can achieve professional-looking and durable sewing projects. Understanding fabric properties, selecting the appropriate tools, and following proper techniques are key to successful and enjoyable sewing experiences.

Chapter 15: Care and Maintenance

15.1: Cleaning and Maintaining Your Sewing Machine

Regular cleaning is crucial for maintaining the optimal performance of your sewing machine. Begin by removing any thread and fabric remnants, using tweezers or a brush to gently dislodge stubborn fibers. Use a soft, lint-free cloth to wipe down the exterior, paying attention to areas where dust and debris tend to accumulate, such as bobbin compartments, needle plates, and tension dials.

For more thorough cleaning, detach the presser foot and needle plate. Use a small brush or compressed air to remove lint and thread from the feed dogs and bobbin case. Lubricate moving parts sparingly, as excessive lubrication can attract dirt and impede performance. Refer to your sewing machine's user manual for specific lubrication points and recommendations.

Maintaining Your Sewing Machine

Proper maintenance ensures that your sewing machine remains in good working order. Regularly inspect the needle and replace it as needed, especially after sewing through thick fabrics or encountering skipped stitches. Ensure that the bobbin is correctly wound and inserted, and adjust the thread tension accordingly.

Check the power cord for any damage or fraying, and replace it if necessary. Clean the lint filter and ventilation ports regularly to prevent overheating and maintain optimal airflow. Store your sewing machine in a dry, dust-free environment when not in use, and cover it with a protective cover to prevent dust and moisture accumulation.

Additional Tips

In addition to regular cleaning and maintenance, here are some additional tips to enhance the longevity of your sewing machine:

Use high-quality thread and needles that are compatible with your machine and the fabrics you are sewing.
Avoid sewing over pins or other metal objects that could damage the needle or machine.

If your sewing machine starts to make unusual noises or perform erratically, stop using it immediately and consult your user manual or a qualified technician.
Regularly clean the bobbin winder, presser foot lever, and other areas where lint and thread tend to accumulate.
Calibrate your sewing machine periodically to ensure accurate stitch length and tension.
Protect your sewing machine from extreme temperatures, humidity, and direct sunlight.

15.2: Storing Fabric and Sewing Supplies

The longevity and quality of your fabric highly depend on proper storage. To maintain the integrity and beauty of your fabrics, it is essential to store them in a cool, dry, and dark place. Avoid exposing them to direct sunlight or excessive heat, as these factors can cause fading, discoloration, and weakening of the fibers.

Ensure that your fabrics are clean and dry before storing them to prevent the growth of mold, mildew, or insects. Fold or roll your fabrics loosely to prevent creases and wrinkles. Avoid using plastic bags for storage, as they trap moisture and can lead to damage. Instead, opt for breathable materials such as muslin, cotton, or acid-free paper.

Organize your fabrics by type, color, or project to make them easily accessible when needed. You can use clear storage bins, drawers, or shelves to keep your fabrics sorted and protected. Regularly inspect your stored fabrics for any signs of damage or pests, and take prompt action to address any issues that arise.

Storing Sewing Supplies

Proper storage of your sewing supplies is equally important to maintain their functionality and longevity. Keep your needles, pins, and other sharp objects in designated containers or pincushions to prevent accidents and damage to your fabrics. Store your threads and yarns in a cool, dry place, away from direct sunlight. Use thread organizers or spools to keep them tangle-free and easily accessible.

Scissors should be stored in a protective case or sheath to prevent dulling or damage. Iron and ironing equipment should be cleaned regularly and stored in a safe, dry place. Keep your sewing machine well-oiled and covered when not in use to protect it from dust and moisture.

Organize your sewing supplies in a logical and accessible manner. Use clear containers, drawers, or shelves to store different categories of supplies, such as notions, tools, and accessories. Label each container or drawer for easy identification. By maintaining a well-organized and clean storage system for your sewing supplies, you can ensure their longevity and enhance your sewing experience.

15.3: Caring for Your Sewing Projects

Store your projects in a cool, dry place. Heat and humidity can damage fabrics and cause colors to fade. Store your projects in a closet or drawer that is away from direct sunlight and heat sources.

Protect your projects from dust and dirt. Dust and dirt can accumulate on your projects over time and cause them to look dull and dingy. To protect your projects, store them in a garment bag or cover them with a sheet when they are not in use.

Handle your projects with care. When handling your projects, be careful not to snag or tear the fabric. Always lift your projects by the seams, and avoid pulling or tugging on the fabric.

Wash your projects according to the care instructions. The care instructions for your projects will vary depending on the type of fabric used. Always follow the care instructions to avoid damaging your projects.

Iron your projects on a low heat setting. Ironing can help to keep your projects looking their best. However, be careful not to iron on too high of a heat setting, as this can damage the fabric.

By following these tips, you can help to ensure that your sewing projects will last for years to come.

15.4: Recycling and Upcycling

Recycling is a common practice in many communities, and there are a variety of recycling programs available. These programs typically collect recyclable materials from homes and businesses, and then sort and process them into new materials. The most commonly recycled materials include paper, plastic, metal, and glass.

Upcycling is a less common practice than recycling, but it is gaining popularity as people become more aware of the importance of sustainability. Upcycling projects can be as simple or complex as you like, and they can be a great way to use old materials in new and creative ways.

One of the benefits of recycling and upcycling is that it can help to reduce waste. When materials are recycled or upcycled, they are kept out of landfills and incinerators. This can help to conserve resources and reduce pollution.

Another benefit of recycling and upcycling is that it can save you money. When you recycle or upcycle, you are essentially reusing materials that you would otherwise have to buy new. This can save you a significant amount of money over time.

In ending, recycling and upcycling can be a fun and creative way to express yourself. There are no limits to what you can create with recycled and upcycled materials. You can use them to make clothing, accessories, home décor, and much more.

If you are looking for ways to reduce your environmental impact and save money, recycling and upcycling are two great options. These practices are easy to do and can make a big difference.

Chapter 16: Inspiration and Resources

16.1: Finding Inspiration for Sewing Projects

Inspiration, the lifeblood of creativity, holds immense significance in the realm of sewing. Unleashing your imagination and discovering innovative ideas are crucial for embarking on captivating sewing projects that resonate with your unique style and aspirations. This one delves into the multifaceted avenues of inspiration, providing a roadmap to ignite your creative spark and propel your sewing journey to new heights.

Embracing the Sensory Canvas

Immerse yourself in the world around you, engaging all your senses to absorb the beauty and wonder that surrounds. Observe the intricate textures of nature, the vibrant hues of flowers, and the architectural wonders of cities. Allow these sensory experiences to permeate your mind, fostering a rich tapestry of ideas that can translate into captivating sewing creations.

The rustling of leaves might inspire a flowing dress, while the glimmering reflections of water could spark a shimmering evening gown.

Tapping into Cultural Heritage

Delve into the depths of history and explore the diverse cultural heritage of sewing. Study the traditional garments and embroidery techniques of different regions, uncovering a wealth of inspiration. From the vibrant colors of Indian saris to the intricate beadwork of Native American moccasins, cultural heritage offers a treasure trove of ideas that can infuse your projects with depth and meaning.

Seeking Inspiration in the Virtual Realm

Harness the boundless possibilities of the internet to fuel your creative engine. Visit sewing blogs, browse online fabric stores, and connect with fellow enthusiasts on social media platforms. Engage with the vibrant sewing community, share ideas, and seek inspiration from the myriad projects showcased online. The vastness of the virtual realm provides endless opportunities to spark your imagination and discover new techniques that will elevate your sewing skills.

Drawing Inspiration from Fashion Trends

Stay abreast of the latest fashion trends, paying attention to the colors, fabrics, and silhouettes that dominate the runways and magazines. Analyze the designs of renowned fashion houses and identify elements that resonate with your personal style. Adapt these trends to your own sewing projects, incorporating elements that complement your wardrobe and reflect your unique aesthetic.

Embarking on the Creative Journey

Inspiration is a journey, not a destination. Embrace the process of exploration, allowing yourself to be open to unexpected sources of inspiration. Keep a sketchbook or journal to capture fleeting ideas and observations. Visit fabric stores and handle different materials, letting their textures and colors ignite your imagination. Attend workshops or classes to learn new techniques and connect with other sewers. The more you engage with the world around you, the richer your reservoir of inspiration will become.

16.2: Online Sewing Communities and Resources

Online sewing communities and resources are a wealth of knowledge and support for sewers of all levels.

These platforms provide a space for sewers to connect with others, share their work, and learn from each other. There are numerous online sewing communities, each with its own unique focus and membership base. Some of the most popular communities include:

Sewing. com: This community offers a wide range of resources, including sewing tips, tutorials, and patterns. It also has a vibrant forum where sewers can connect with others and ask questions.

ThreadBanger: This community is focused on modern sewing and quilting. It features a variety of articles, tutorials, and patterns, as well as a forum where members can share their work and connect with others.

Craftster: This community is dedicated to all things crafts, including sewing. It offers a variety of resources, including tutorials, patterns, and a forum where members can share their work and connect with others.

In addition to online sewing communities, there are also a number of online resources that can be helpful for sewers. These resources include:

Sewing websites: These websites offer a variety of

information on sewing, including tutorials, patterns, and tips. Some of the most popular sewing websites include:

AllFreeSewing: This website offers a wide range of free sewing patterns, tutorials, and tips.
Craftsy: This website offers online sewing classes and workshops, as well as a variety of sewing patterns and supplies.
Sew Mama Sew: This website offers a variety of sewing tutorials, patterns, and tips.

Sewing blogs: Sewing blogs are a great way to learn about new sewing techniques, patterns, and products. Some of the most popular sewing blogs include:

Sew Can She: This blog features a variety of sewing tutorials, patterns, and tips.
The Purl Bee: This blog features a variety of sewing tutorials, patterns, and tips, as well as interviews with sewing experts.
Sew Much Ado: This blog features a variety of sewing tutorials, patterns, and tips, as well as reviews of sewing products.

Online sewing communities and resources can be a valuable asset for sewers of all levels. These platforms provide a wealth of knowledge, support, and inspiration. By taking advantage of these resources, sewers can learn new techniques, expand their skills, and connect with other sewers.

16.3: Local Sewing Classes and Workshops

Whether you're a complete novice eager to master the basics or a seasoned sewer seeking to refine your craft, local sewing classes cater to a wide range of skill levels and interests. Beginner-friendly classes introduce the fundamentals of sewing, covering essential techniques such as threading the machine, selecting fabrics, and constructing simple garments. More advanced workshops delve into specialized areas such as pattern drafting, garment construction, and intricate embellishments.

The benefits of attending local sewing classes extend far beyond the technical skills acquired. These classes foster a sense of community and shared passion, providing a space for sewers to connect, exchange ideas, and inspire each other. The camaraderie and support found within these groups can be incredibly motivating and help participants stay engaged in their sewing journey.

In addition to the traditional classroom setting, many

local sewing classes and workshops are now available online. These virtual classes offer flexibility and convenience, allowing participants to learn at their own pace and from the comfort of their own homes. Online classes often feature interactive video lessons, downloadable patterns, and access to online forums where students can connect with instructors and fellow classmates.

Whether you opt for in-person or online classes, the key to maximizing your learning experience is to choose a class that aligns with your skill level and interests. Research local sewing schools and community centers to find classes that fit your schedule and learning style. Don't hesitate to reach out to instructors with any questions or concerns to ensure the class is a good fit for you.

Attending local sewing classes and workshops is an investment in your creative journey. These classes provide a wealth of knowledge, support, and inspiration to help you develop your skills, foster your passion for sewing, and create beautiful and meaningful projects that will bring you joy for years to come.

16.4: Sewing Books and Magazines

Sewing books and magazines provide a wealth of inspiration, instruction, and resources for aspiring and experienced sewists alike. They offer a diverse range of content, including:

Step-by-step tutorials: These detailed instructions guide readers through the process of creating specific sewing projects, from basic garments to intricate home décor items.

Patterns: Sewing books and magazines often include patterns that readers can use to create their own garments and accessories. These patterns come in a variety of sizes and styles, catering to different skill levels and preferences.

Inspiration galleries: Beautiful photography and inspiring stories showcase the work of talented sewists, providing a visual feast of ideas and motivation.

Fabric and materials guides: These resources help readers understand the different types of fabrics and materials available, their properties, and how to choose the best options for their projects.

Expert advice: Sewing books and magazines often feature articles written by sewing experts, offering tips, tricks, and troubleshooting guidance to help readers improve their skills.

Choosing Sewing Books and Magazines

When selecting sewing books and magazines, there are several factors to consider:

Skill level: Choose publications that are appropriate for your skill level. If you're a beginner, look for books with clear instructions and step-by-step photos.

Interests: Consider your sewing interests and choose publications that focus on the types of projects you're interested in making.

Style: Different sewing books and magazines have their own unique style. Browse through several publications to find ones that resonate with your personal taste.

Reputation: Look for publications that are published by reputable companies or written by experienced sewists. This helps ensure that the information is accurate and reliable.

Online resources: Many sewing books and magazines also offer online resources, such as downloadable patterns, tutorials, and community forums. Consider this when selecting a publication.

By incorporating sewing books and magazines into their learning and practice, sewists can enhance their skills, expand their creativity, and stay up-to-date with the latest trends and techniques in the sewing world.

Chapter 17: Developing Your Sewing Skills

17.1: Practice Makes Perfect

Moreover, practice fosters confidence and reduces hesitation. As individuals repeatedly engage in sewing projects, they develop a sense of competence and self-assurance. This newfound confidence empowers them to tackle more challenging projects and experiment with different fabrics, patterns, and embellishments.

Additionally, practice provides opportunities for self-evaluation and improvement. By observing the outcomes of their work, sewers can identify areas where they need to improve. Whether it's fine-tuning stitch length, mastering seam finishing techniques, or refining pattern matching skills, regular practice allows individuals to pinpoint and address areas for growth.

It's important to note that practice should be deliberate and focused. Mindlessly repeating tasks without paying attention to technique and accuracy will not yield significant improvement. Instead, sewers should approach practice with a goal-oriented mindset, focusing on specific aspects they wish to enhance. This targeted approach ensures that practice time is utilized effectively and leads to tangible results.

Furthermore, practice should be enjoyable and engaging. If sewing becomes a chore, it's less likely that individuals will stick with it long enough to reap its benefits. Finding projects that spark joy and ignite creativity can make the practice process more enjoyable and sustainable.

17.2: Taking on More Challenging Projects

As a beginner sewer, it's tempting to stick to familiar patterns and projects that provide a sense of comfort and predictability. However, to truly develop your sewing skills and unlock your creative potential, it's essential to embrace more challenging projects that push your boundaries. While stepping outside of your comfort zone may initially evoke feelings of trepidation, it's a necessary step towards becoming a skilled and versatile seamster or seamstress.

Challenging projects offer a unique opportunity to expand your knowledge, hone your techniques, and develop problem-solving abilities. By tackling projects with unfamiliar materials, complex construction methods, or intricate designs, you'll be forced to think critically, research new techniques, and experiment with different approaches. This immersive learning experience not only enhances your technical proficiency but also fosters a deeper understanding of the sewing process as a whole.

Moreover, challenging projects ignite creativity and inspire innovation. When faced with obstacles or unexpected challenges, you'll be forced to tap into your imagination and find innovative solutions. This can lead to the development of unique design elements, novel construction techniques, and a personal style that sets your work apart. By embracing the challenge, you'll unlock a wellspring of creativity that will enrich both your sewing journey and the finished products you create.

The pursuit of challenging projects also fosters a sense of accomplishment and personal growth. When you successfully complete a complex or demanding project, you'll not only have a tangible product to show for it but also an immense sense of satisfaction and pride in your achievements. This positive reinforcement fuels your motivation and encourages you to continue pushing your boundaries and exploring new frontiers in sewing.

Approaching challenging projects requires a mindset shift from avoidance to excitement. Instead of viewing them as obstacles, embrace them as opportunities for growth and learning. Break down the project into smaller, manageable steps, and approach each step with a positive attitude and a willingness to experiment. Remember that mistakes are an inherent part of the learning process, and don't be afraid to ask for help or seek guidance from experienced sewers.

As you embark on more challenging sewing projects, keep a record of your progress, document the techniques you learn, and reflect on your successes and challenges. This personal sewing journal will serve as a valuable resource, tracking your growth as a seamster or seamstress and providing inspiration for future projects. Embrace the journey of mastery, and let challenging projects ignite your passion for sewing and unlock your creative potential.

17.3: Experimenting with Different Techniques

Experimentation is a crucial aspect of mastering any craft, and sewing is no exception. By trying out different techniques, you'll not only expand your skills but also discover your personal preferences and creative style. Start by experimenting with various stitches. Each stitch has a unique look and purpose, so try them out on scrap fabric to see how they behave. Play with the tension and length settings to further customize the appearance of your stitches. Experiment with different fabrics. The type of fabric you choose will significantly impact the final outcome of your project. Try sewing with a range of fabrics, such as cotton, silk, linen, and denim, to understand their different properties. Consider the drape, texture, and weight of each fabric and how they might affect your project. Experiment with embellishments. Embellishments can add a touch of personality and style to your sewing projects. Try using beads, sequins, embroidery, or ribbons to decorate your creations. Don't be afraid to mix and match different embellishments to create unique and eye-catching effects. Experiment with different patterns. Patterns provide a framework for your sewing projects, but they don't have to be set in stone. Try modifying patterns to suit your personal taste or to accommodate specific fabrics. Experiment with different construction techniques. There are many different ways to construct a garment or accessory. Try out different techniques, such as French seams, flat felled seams, or bias binding, to see which ones you prefer and which ones are most appropriate for your project. Experimentation is an ongoing process. The more you sew, the more opportunities you'll have to try out new techniques and refine your skills. Don't be afraid to experiment with different materials, colors, and ideas. The beauty of sewing lies in its endless possibilities for creativity and self-expression.

17.4: Finding Your Sewing Niche

Identifying a niche in sewing involves exploring your interests, skills, and target market to establish a specialized area of focus. This strategic approach allows you to cater to a specific audience, showcase your unique abilities, and establish yourself as an expert in a particular sewing domain.

To find your sewing niche, consider your personal preferences and interests. What types of sewing projects bring you joy and fulfillment. Do you prefer garment construction, home décor, accessories, or a specific technique like embroidery or quilting. Pinpoint your passions and areas of expertise, as they will serve as the foundation for your niche.

Next, assess your skills and identify your strengths and weaknesses. Evaluate your proficiency in various sewing techniques, fabrics, and design elements. Determine which areas you excel in and which require further development. By understanding your skill set, you can tailor your niche to align with your capabilities and avoid projects that may be beyond your current abilities.

Understanding your target market is crucial for defining your sewing niche. Consider who you want to reach with your sewing creations. Are you targeting fellow sewists, fashion enthusiasts, home decorators, or a specific demographic group. Research your potential customers, their interests, and the types of sewing products or services they seek. By aligning your niche with the needs of your target market, you increase the likelihood of attracting a loyal customer base.

Once you have explored your interests, skills, and target market, start narrowing down your niche. Consider focusing on a particular style, such as vintage, bohemian, or minimalist. Alternatively, you could specialize in a specific garment type, like bridal gowns, evening wear, or children's clothing. You might also consider offering specialized services, such as custom alterations, upholstery, or sewing classes. By defining your niche, you establish a clear identity and direction for your sewing endeavors.

Chapter 18: Sewing for the Future

18.1: Exploring Different Sewing Careers

The world of sewing extends beyond the confines of personal projects and hobbyist pursuits. A plethora of professional opportunities await those with a passion for needle and thread, offering diverse paths to explore. Whether your interests lie in the realm of fashion, textiles, or education, the sewing industry presents an array of fulfilling careers.

Fashion's Creative Arena

The fashion industry is a vibrant hub for talented sewers and designers. Fashion designers conceptualize and create garments, translating their artistic visions into tangible pieces. They work closely with fabric, selecting the perfect materials to bring their designs to life. Pattern makers translate these designs into precise patterns, ensuring garments fit flawlessly. Sample sewers meticulously craft prototypes to evaluate designs and fine-tune details. Production sewers work diligently to produce garments on a larger scale, ensuring that the final products meet the high standards of the fashion house.

Textile Exploration and Innovation

The textile industry offers another exciting avenue for sewing professionals. Textile designers create unique fabrics, experimenting with different fibers, textures, and patterns. Textile engineers focus on the technical aspects of textiles, ensuring they meet industry standards for durability, comfort, and performance. Fabric analysts assess the quality of textiles, ensuring they meet specific requirements. Colorists play a crucial role in developing and matching colors, creating the vibrant hues that adorn our garments and home textiles.

Education and Inspiration

For those passionate about sharing their love of sewing, the field of education offers a rewarding path. Sewing teachers guide students of all ages, from beginners to aspiring professionals. They develop lesson plans, provide instruction, and assess student progress. Sewing educators can work in schools, community centers, or private studios, fostering a love of the craft in future generations. Sewing authors and bloggers share their knowledge and expertise through books, articles, and online platforms, inspiring others to explore the world of sewing.

Diverse Opportunities for Skilled Sewers

The sewing industry encompasses a vast array of specialized roles, each offering its own unique challenges and rewards. Alteration specialists adjust and repair garments to ensure a perfect fit. Upholsterers transform furniture with new fabrics, restoring old pieces and creating custom designs. Costume designers bring characters to life through their creations, working in the worlds of theater, film, and television. Quilters create intricate and beautiful works of art, using their skills to preserve memories and add warmth to homes.

The field of sewing offers a wealth of career opportunities for those with a love of the craft. From fashion design to textile innovation and education, there is a path to suit every passion and skill set. Whether you aspire to create beautiful garments, explore the technical aspects of textiles, or share your knowledge with others, the sewing industry welcomes you with open arms. Embrace the endless possibilities that await and embark on a fulfilling journey as a skilled sewer.

18.2: Starting Your Own Sewing Business

Embarking on the entrepreneurial journey as a seamstress requires a comprehensive understanding of the business landscape and a meticulous approach to planning. To establish a successful sewing business, one must carefully consider market analysis, business structure, financial planning, marketing strategies, and operational efficiency.

A thorough market analysis is crucial to determine the viability of a sewing business in the target area. This involves identifying the potential customer base, understanding their needs and preferences, and assessing the level of competition. A well-defined target market will help focus marketing efforts and tailor products and services accordingly.

Choosing the appropriate business structure is essential for legal and financial considerations. Factors to consider include the number of owners, liability exposure, and tax implications. The options range from sole proprietorship to limited liability companies (LLCs) and corporations, each with its advantages and disadvantages.

Financial planning is paramount to ensure the long-term sustainability of the business. This includes determining startup costs, estimating operating expenses, and projecting revenue streams. A detailed budget will help track expenses, manage cash flow, and make informed financial decisions. Accessing financing options, such as small business loans or grants, may be necessary to cover initial expenses.

Developing a comprehensive marketing strategy is vital for attracting and retaining customers. This involves identifying target audiences, creating a unique brand identity, and implementing effective marketing channels. Online presence, social media marketing, and networking events can be effective ways to reach potential customers and showcase products and services.

Operational efficiency is essential for maximizing productivity and profitability. This involves optimizing workflow, implementing inventory management systems, and establishing quality control measures. Streamlining processes, investing in technology, and partnering with reliable suppliers can help improve efficiency and reduce operating costs. By carefully considering these factors and developing a comprehensive plan, aspiring seamstresses can lay the foundation for a successful and sustainable enterprise.

18.3: The Future of Sewing: Trends and Technology

One of the most prominent trends shaping the future of sewing is the rise of smart textiles. These fabrics are imbued with embedded sensors, microcontrollers, and other electronic components, unlocking a world of possibilities for interactive and responsive garments. Imagine clothing that can monitor your vital signs, adjust its temperature to your body, or even change its color and texture on demand. Smart textiles are poised to revolutionize the fashion industry, creating garments that are not only aesthetically pleasing but also highly functional.

Another key trend driving the future of sewing is the advent of 3D printing technology. This innovative approach to manufacturing has the potential to revolutionize the way garments are designed and produced. With 3D printing, designers can create complex and intricate patterns that would be impossible to achieve using traditional sewing techniques. Moreover, 3D printing allows for the creation of customized garments tailored to the individual wearer's measurements and preferences.

In addition to these technological advancements, the future of sewing is also influenced by emerging trends in sustainability and ethical consumption. Consumers are increasingly demanding garments that are produced in an environmentally friendly and socially responsible manner. This has led to a growing emphasis on the use of sustainable materials, such as organic cotton and recycled fabrics. Moreover, ethical considerations, such as fair labor practices and transparency in the supply chain, are becoming increasingly important to consumers.

The convergence of these trends and technologies is poised to create a future of sewing that is both innovative and sustainable. Smart textiles, 3D printing, and a focus on sustainability will empower sewers to create garments that are not only beautiful but also functional, ethical, and environmentally friendly. The future of sewing is filled with exciting possibilities, and it is up to the sewers of tomorrow to embrace these advancements and shape the craft in new and innovative ways.

18.4: Sharing Your Sewing Passion

Consider organizing workshops or classes tailored to various skill levels. These gatherings provide a nurturing environment for aspiring sewers to master fundamental techniques, gain confidence, and explore their creativity under your expert guidance. You could also establish a local sewing club or join existing groups to foster a vibrant community of sewers. Regular meetups, workshops, and exhibitions offer invaluable opportunities to exchange ideas, learn from one another, and showcase your collective talents.

Social media platforms have emerged as powerful tools for connecting with sewing enthusiasts across geographical boundaries. Create a dedicated sewing blog or establish a presence on popular social media platforms. Share your sewing adventures, tutorials, and inspiring projects with a global audience. By engaging with fellow sewers online, you can cultivate a sense of community, inspire others, and gain valuable feedback on your own work.

Beyond formal settings, embrace every opportunity to share your passion for sewing with friends, family, and acquaintances. Offer to mend or alter clothing, create custom gifts, or organize informal sewing sessions. By demonstrating the joy and practicality of sewing, you can sow seeds of inspiration in the minds of those around you. Encourage them to explore this rewarding craft, providing support and guidance as they embark on their own sewing journeys.

Remember, sharing your sewing passion is not merely about teaching others a skill but about fostering a sense of community, creativity, and empowerment. By creating opportunities for connection, collaboration, and inspiration, you can ignite a love for sewing in others and contribute to the vibrant tapestry of this timeless craft.

Chapter 19: Glossary of Terms

19.1: Common Sewing Terminology

Accuracy

Precision and correctness in sewing are crucial for achieving a professional-looking finish. Accuracy refers to the exactness of measurements, seam allowances, and pattern placement. Maintaining accuracy throughout the sewing process ensures that the garment or project fits well and meets the desired specifications.

Bias

Bias refers to the diagonal direction of a fabric, running at a 45-degree angle to the lengthwise and crosswise grainlines. Cutting and sewing fabric on the bias allows it to stretch more easily, creating drapes, gathers, and other effects. However, bias-cut fabrics are more prone to stretching out of shape if not handled carefully.

Dart

A dart is a triangular or wedge-shaped piece of fabric sewn into a seam to create shape and fit. Darts are commonly used to contour areas such as the bust, waist, and hips, providing a more flattering fit. The depth and length of the dart determine the amount of shaping and fullness achieved.

Facings

Facings are pieces of fabric sewn around the edges of openings such as necklines, armholes, and hems. They provide a clean and finished look, prevent fraying, and reinforce the garment. Facings are usually made from a lightweight, fusible interfacing or a separate piece of fabric.

Grain

The grain of a fabric refers to the direction of the threads woven together. The lengthwise grain runs parallel to the selvage, while the crosswise grain runs perpendicular to it. Understanding the grain is essential for cutting and sewing patterns correctly, as it determines the stability, stretch, and drape of the fabric.

Interfacing

Interfacing is a non-woven fabric used to reinforce and add structure to specific areas of a garment or project. It is available in various weights and types, depending on the desired effect. Interfacing can be sewn or fused to the fabric, providing additional strength, stability, and shape retention.

Seam

A seam is the line of stitches that joins two or more pieces of fabric together. There are various types of seams, each with its own purpose and appearance. Common seams include plain seams, French seams, and serged seams. The choice of seam depends on the fabric, the seam allowance, and the desired finish.

Selvage

Selvage is the finished edge of a woven fabric that prevents unraveling. It is typically firmer and denser than the rest of the fabric and is identified by the small, evenly spaced stitches running along the edge. When working with fabric, it is important to pay attention to the selvage to ensure proper grain alignment and to avoid fraying.

Underlining

Underlining involves attaching a layer of lightweight fabric to the inside of a garment or project to provide extra support and opacity. It is commonly used with sheer or lightweight fabrics to give them more body and to prevent them from becoming see-through. Underlining also helps to smooth out wrinkles and improve the overall drape of the garment.

Zipper

A zipper is a closure used in garments and accessories to fasten openings. It consists of two interlocking rows of teeth that slide together when the slider is pulled up. Zippers are available in various lengths, styles, and colors, and can be sewn into seams, inserted into zippers, or used as decorative elements.

19.2: Fabric Types and Properties

Fabrics, the foundation of any sewing project, are woven, knitted, or nonwoven textiles available in a vast array of materials, textures, and patterns. Woven fabrics, created by interlacing perpendicular yarns, exhibit stability and durability. Knitted fabrics, formed by looping yarns together, offer elasticity and drape. Nonwoven fabrics, produced by bonding fibers together without weaving or knitting, provide versatility and functionality.

The choice of fabric depends on the intended use of the garment or accessory. Natural fibers, such as cotton, linen, and wool, are breathable, absorbent, and eco-friendly. Synthetic fibers, like polyester, nylon, and spandex, are wrinkle-resistant, durable, and moisture-wicking. Blends of natural and synthetic fibers combine the advantages of both, offering versatility and specific performance characteristics.

Fabric Properties

Understanding fabric properties is essential for selecting the appropriate material for a project. Weight refers to the thickness and density of the fabric, ranging from lightweight sheers to heavy canvas. Drape describes how the fabric falls and moves, influenced by its weight and fiber content. Texture refers to the surface feel of the fabric, from smooth satin to rough tweed.

Opacity determines how much light passes through the fabric, categorized as sheer, semi-transparent, or opaque. Stretch refers to the fabric's ability to expand and contract, important for garments requiring flexibility. Shrinkage potential indicates how much the fabric may shrink after laundering, affecting garment sizing. Care instructions provide guidance on washing, drying, and ironing to maintain the fabric's integrity.

Choosing the Right Fabric

Selecting the right fabric involves considering the intended use, desired look, and personal preferences. For everyday garments, cotton, linen, or polyester blends offer comfort, breathability, and wrinkle resistance. For formal occasions, silk, satin, or lace provide elegance and drape. For activewear, spandex or moisture-wicking fabrics ensure flexibility and comfort.

Matching the fabric to the project is crucial. Lightweight fabrics like voile or chiffon are ideal for blouses and summer dresses. Medium-weight fabrics like cotton poplin or chambray are suitable for shirts, skirts, and pants. Heavy-weight fabrics like denim or canvas are ideal for jeans, bags, and jackets. By understanding fabric types and properties, aspiring sewers can make informed choices and create garments and accessories that meet their needs and desires.

19.3: Sewing Machine Parts and Functions

A sewing machine is a mechanical device used to sew fabric and other materials together with thread. Sewing machines can be either manual or powered by electricity. They come in a variety of sizes and styles, from small portable models to large industrial machines.

The basic parts of a sewing machine include the head, the bed, the needle, the bobbin, and the thread. The head of the machine contains the motor, the gears, and the tension discs. The bed of the machine supports the fabric as it is being sewn. The needle pierces the fabric and carries the thread through it. The bobbin holds the lower thread, which is wound around it. The thread is pulled through the fabric by the needle and the bobbin thread, creating a stitch.

In addition to these basic parts, sewing machines may also have a number of other features, such as a presser foot, a feed dog, and a stitch selector. The presser foot holds the fabric in place as it is being sewn. The feed dog moves the fabric through the machine. The stitch selector allows the user to choose the type of stitch that will be used.

Sewing machines are versatile tools that can be used to create a wide variety of projects, from simple repairs to elaborate garments. With a little practice, anyone can learn to use a sewing machine and create their own beautiful sewn creations.

Here are some of the most common sewing machine parts and their functions:

Head: The head of the sewing machine contains the motor, the gears, and the tension discs.
Bed: The bed of the sewing machine supports the fabric as it is being sewn.
Needle: The needle pierces the fabric and carries the thread through it.
Bobbin: The bobbin holds the lower thread, which is wound around it.
Thread: The thread is pulled through the fabric by the needle and the bobbin thread, creating a stitch.
Presser foot: The presser foot holds the fabric in place as it is being sewn.
Feed dog: The feed dog moves the fabric through the machine.
Stitch selector: The stitch selector allows the user to choose the type of stitch that will be used.

In addition to these basic parts, sewing machines may also have a number of other features, such as:

Buttonhole maker: A buttonhole maker is a special attachment that can be used to create buttonholes in fabric.

Blind hemmer: A blind hemmer is a special attachment that can be used to create blind hems in fabric.

Zipper foot: A zipper foot is a special attachment that can be used to sew zippers into fabric.

Overlock foot: An overlock foot is a special attachment that can be used to create overlocked seams in fabric.

Chapter 20: Conclusion

20.1: The Joy of Sewing

Sewing transcends the realm of mere fabric manipulation; it is an art form that intertwines self-expression, practicality, and a profound sense of joy. Embarking on a sewing journey is akin to embarking on a creative odyssey, where the limitations are boundless and the possibilities are endless. With each stitch, a tapestry of dreams and aspirations unravels, transforming the mundane into the extraordinary.

Sewing empowers individuals to breathe life into their designs, giving tangible form to their imagination. Whether it be a whimsical quilt, a flowing dress, or a cozy blanket, each creation becomes a reflection of the sewer's unique style and personality. The act of sewing cultivates a sense of accomplishment, fostering a belief in one's own abilities and nurturing a spirit of creativity that extends beyond the sewing room.

Beyond its aesthetic and creative benefits, sewing also serves a practical purpose, enabling individuals to mend, alter, and personalize their clothing and household items. By mastering this versatile craft, individuals gain a sense of independence and self-reliance, becoming empowered to maintain and enhance their belongings. The act of sewing transforms the mundane into the meaningful, imbuing everyday objects with a touch of artistry and individuality.

Moreover, sewing fosters a sense of community and connection. Whether sharing tips with fellow sewers or joining a sewing group, the craft brings people together, fostering a spirit of collaboration and mutual support. The shared experience of creating something beautiful and functional creates an unbreakable bond among sewers, transcending geographical boundaries and uniting them in a global tapestry of creativity. It empowers individuals to express themselves, cultivate their abilities, and connect with others through the shared passion of creating something extraordinary. As one embarks on this transformative journey, the joy of sewing will permeate every aspect of their life, enriching their creativity, enhancing their practicality, and fostering a sense of community that transcends the boundaries of fabric and thread.

20.2: Continuing Your Sewing Journey

Moreover, consider venturing into the world of online resources, where a wealth of tutorials, patterns, and inspiration can be found. Numerous websites and YouTube channels offer comprehensive guidance, from beginner-friendly projects to more advanced techniques. By immersing yourself in these online communities, you can access a vast reservoir of knowledge and connect with a global network of passionate sewers.

As you progress, don't be afraid to experiment with different fabrics, patterns, and embellishments. Experimentation is the lifeblood of creativity, and it's through trial and error that you will discover what truly resonates with your personal style. Embrace the unexpected, and don't hesitate to mix and match techniques to create one-of-a-kind pieces that reflect your unique vision.

Remember, the beauty of sewing lies in its versatility. Whether you aspire to craft garments, home décor, or personalized gifts, the possibilities are boundless. Let your imagination soar, and don't be afraid to explore beyond the confines of traditional patterns. With each project you undertake, you will not only hone your skills but also cultivate a deeper appreciation for the artistry and practicality of this timeless craft.

As your proficiency grows, you may find yourself drawn to specialized areas of sewing, such as quilting, embroidery, or tailoring. Consider delving into these niche disciplines through workshops, books, or online courses. By specializing in a particular aspect of sewing, you can refine your techniques, expand your knowledge base, and create truly exceptional pieces.

Never underestimate the power of seeking guidance when you encounter challenges. Whether it's a seasoned seamstress, a sewing group, or an online forum, don't hesitate to ask for help when you need it. The sewing community is renowned for its warmth and camaraderie, and there is always someone willing to lend a helping hand or offer words of encouragement.

Lastly, remember that sewing is a journey, not a destination. Embrace the process, celebrate your progress, and don't be discouraged by occasional setbacks. With dedication, perseverance, and a love for the craft, you will continue to grow as a sewer, creating beautiful, meaningful, and enduring pieces that bring joy to you and those around you.

20.3: Sharing Your Creations with the World

The realm of sewing, like many creative endeavors, is a vibrant tapestry woven from countless individual threads. The act of sharing your creations with the world is not merely a display of pride but a profound expression of connection, community, and inspiration. As you embark on this journey, you become an ambassador for your craft, fostering a shared appreciation for the art of sewing.

Social media platforms, with their vast reach and instantaneity, offer a boundless arena for showcasing your creations. From Instagram's vibrant feed to Pinterest's curated boards, each platform presents unique opportunities to engage with a global audience. By capturing stunning photographs of your finished projects, you invite others to immerse themselves in your creative vision, sparking admiration and inspiring their own sewing endeavors.

Embracing Vulnerability: Growth Through Feedback

Sharing your creations is not just about basking in the glory of compliments; it's also about embracing vulnerability and seeking constructive feedback. By actively listening to the insights and suggestions of others, you embark on a path of continuous growth. Each interaction becomes an opportunity to refine your techniques, expand your knowledge, and unlock new possibilities within your craft.

Moreover, sharing your creations opens doors to collaborations and partnerships with fellow sewists. Through online forums and social media groups, you can connect with like-minded individuals who share your passion for sewing. Together, you can exchange ideas, learn from each other's experiences, and embark on joint projects that push the boundaries of your creativity.

Inspiring the Next Generation: Nurturing a Creative Legacy

The act of sharing your sewing creations has a profound impact beyond your immediate circle. By inspiring others to take up the needle and thread, you contribute to the preservation and growth of this timeless craft. Whether it's through workshops, online tutorials, or simply showcasing your own creations, you become a beacon of inspiration for aspiring sewists, encouraging them to explore their creativity and discover the joy of self-expression through sewing.

As you continue your sewing journey, remember that sharing your creations is an integral part of the creative process. Embrace the opportunity to connect with the world, inspire others, and nurture the future of sewing.

With each stitch you share, you weave a vibrant tapestry that celebrates the transformative power of creativity.

Made in the USA
Monee, IL
28 December 2025

40540109R00115